THE HISTORY OF PURNELL & SONS LTD.

AND

THE BRITISH PRINTING CORPORATION

THE HISTORY OF PURNELL & SONS LTD.

AND

THE BRITISH PRINTING CORPORATION

BY

TERRY GOODMAN

(TG)

The History of Purnell & Sons Ltd. and the British Printing Corporation
First Published 2004 by Terry Goodman

© Terry Goodman, 2004

The moral right of the author has been asserted

ISBN:0-9547241-0-0

Printed and bound in Great Britain by Creative Print & Design (Wales) Ltd.

CONTENTS

FOREWORD

I often thought it strange that the small, village printer of Purnell & Sons Ltd., that grew to become The British Printing Corporation, had no recorded official history as had several of the companies that Purnells took over and joined in the 1960's. In fact, some companies like Waterlows and Hazell Watson & Viney could boast more than one written history. It is for this reason alone that I have attempted to put on paper, perhaps inadequately, the result of years of research into old records, photographs and talks with "old timers", for the benefit of all those that worked for Purnells in whatever capacity.

The book features two main families, the Purnells and the Harveys, the former family started the business and the latter took it from village printer status to the largest printing group in Britain in a thirty-year period, from 1935 to 1965.

Above all, the book is mainly about books and the people who made them. .

Terry Goodman. Timsbury, April 2001.

ACKNOWLEDGEMENTS

It was in 1978 that I mentioned to Donald McIntosh, the Managing Director of Purnells, that the company should have had a history of its development written by now, in typical Mac style, he replied, "Well write it then". I have to say; that without the support of the directors, managers and workforce in general, the gathering together of photographs, documents, anything of historical interests in fact, the writing would have been an impossible task.

Special thanks are due to my late departed friend Maurice Harvey who had the foresight to save bag loads of early documents, nearly all soaking wet, some beyond salvage, that had been stored in the corridors and odd corners of the house at Park Corner.

Wendy Walker for allowing me to browse through the old copies of the 'Somerset Guardian', and for printing some extracts from the book in 'The Bath and West Evening Chronicle', in 1984.

David Bailey, Company Director and Chairman of the Cricket Club, for the scrapbooks he had kept and the photographs. Donald McIntosh, Bob Wilshire, Tony Wilmot, John Brimble and the late Roly Harrison for their input on the Budwigs and litho-platemaking. George Lambert for his donation of photographs that covered practically every retirement presentation of the Composing Department in the last 50 years.

I have received dozens of individual photographs from the staff in all departments, too numerous to name, but whose contributions have all gone towards making a more complete picture of this history of a very important printing company. Jane Bell and Anthea Green ably executed the typing of the early draft paragraphs and they have my hearty thanks; without the enormous help of my friend Deborah Clement on computer type setting, the book would never have been finished; and above all my friend Keith Jeffery, without whose practical help and encouragement this book would have not been published.

LIST OF ILLUSTRATIONS

BIBLIOGRAPHY

The annual report and accounts for Purnell and Sons Ltd., Hazell Sun Ltd., Waterlow Ltd., BPC Ltd., BPCC Ltd., the House Magazine of Waterlows (Wands), the BPC Group Magazine Impressions, the National Daily Press financial reports and The Somerset Guardian.

The Memorandum and Articles of Association of Paulton Holdings Limited, dated 8th. April 1936 and the Purnell and Sons Limited Prospectus, dated 20th.March 1935.

Property plans and details come from the 1935 and 1964 reports conducted by Leopold Farmer and Sons, surveyors and valuers, of Gresham Street, London.

The BPE photographs are taken from the 1911 edition of that fine printer's annual, The Penrose Annual.

CHAPTER ONE

PURNELL & SONS: THE EARLY HISTORY

The Purnell family of printers, who lived at Paulton and the surrounding area, can be traced through the population census records that are taken every 10 years, beginning in 1841. It is well known that the first census had a few flaws and was not entirely accurate, but subsequent ones improved progressively. Other records, particularly religious ones, of weddings, christenings, and deaths, held in churches, chapels and by the civil authorities have all helped in trying to trace as accurately as possible the Purnell family of printers that formed the foundation of the largest printing group in Britain in 1964

The 1841 census records a certain Charles Hewitt, aged 26 years, his wife Maria, aged 21 years, their child Sarah, aged 10 months. Their address is given in Paulton as the Pithay; Charles Hewitt's occupation is given as Printer and Bookbinder. Maria Hewitt was the daughter of George Purnell and the sister of Charles Dando Purnell. The 1851 census returns for Paulton do not record the Hewitts, but show that Alfred Purnell and Henry Herbert Purnell, sons of George Purnell, Coal-Agent were living at 28 the Pithay in Paulton with their mother Mary Maria Purnell, aged 64 years. Alfred Purnell gave his occupation as a Master Printer and Bookbinder, and Henry Herbert Purnell gave his as a Printer's Compositor. The same 1851 census shows Charles Dando Purnell, aged 28 years, Coal-Agent, his wife Maria, aged 25 years, were living at the Batch in Paulton, together with their children George Henry Purnell, aged one year and Charles Herbert Purnell, aged four months.

It can be seen that after the passage of another 10 years the Purnell family had moved home yet again, because the 1861 census returns show that Charles Dando Purnell was now living at 42 High Park Paulton with his increased family as follows: George Henry, aged 11. Charles Herbert, aged 10. Rebecca aged 8. Toni H, aged 4. Arthur, aged 1. Henry Herbert Purnell had moved with his mother Mary Maria, now aged 74, to 46 High Park Paulton.

The High Park location was where the printing works developed over the following years, not only in Paulton but with branches in Midsomer Norton and Radstock as well, albeit on a smaller scale than at Paulton.

The Purnell family also grew at High Park Corner, as it became known; Clifford John Purnell was born at High Park Corner to his parents Charles Dando Purnell and Maria Purnell in 1865, and became one of the main founders and Chairman of the business when it became Purnell and Sons Ltd. in1935, but more of this later.

A 1912 photograph of Purnell & Sons at Park Corner Paulton.

A 1920's photograph of Purnell & Sons at Park Corner, Paulton. Note the alterations to the neighbouring buildings, compared to the previous photograph.

It will have been noticed that George Purnell and his son Charles Dando Purnell were Coal Agents in Paulton according to the census returns for 1841-51.

The coal mining industry was already in decline in Paulton at this time and the last pit was destined to close in 1864. It is very obvious that Charles Dando Purnell had to seek other, alternative means of supporting his family and when his sister married a printer and bookbinder in 1839, the embryo of the printing firm of C. D. Purnell was established.

The local industry mainly comprised of agriculture, the Somerset Coalfield companies, iron- founding, boot manufacturing, the fledgling railway companies and, as far as printers were concerned, the churches, chapels and the local Council Unions. All these concerns required stationery, posters and receipts etc. and this was the When Post-cards were permitted to carry pictures, collecting them became a craze and the printers all benefited from this including Purnells who had their own range of local views, mainly of an industrial nature.

THE PURNELL FAMILY

George Purnell. Born 1781 and married Mary Maria Dando from Camerton in 1809, she was born in 1787.

Children: John Christened 1810, Anne Christened 1813, George Christened 1814, James Christened 1816, Samuel Christened 1818, Charles Dando christened 1822.

Maria Dando Purnell, b. 1820, married Charles John Hewitt in 1839; he was a printer and bookbinder according to the 1841 census returns. This was where her bother Charles Dando Purnell got his first practical experience of the printing trade.

Followed by the following brothers:

Walter	1825
Joseph	1827
Alfred	1829
Henry Herbert	1832

Charles Dando Purnell

Charles Dando Purnell. (1822-1913)
Married Maria Killen (1826-1895)
Their Children:
Arthur (Married Charlotte)
Willie (Married Alice)
George Henry b.1849
Charles Herbert b.1850 (Married Louise)
Rebecca Rowena b.1852 (Married Joseph Flook)
Clifford John (1865-1971)

Clifford John Purnell (1865-1971)
His father handed the day-to-day management of the business to him in 1885; he was only 20 years old.
He became Chairman of the Company in 1935, when it became Purnell & Sons Ltd.
He retired from the Company in 1945
Aged 80 years old but kept an active interest in the business right up to his death in 1971, aged 106 years.
His working life spanned 65 years spent entirely at Paulton and he died in the same house that he was born in, at Park Corner Paulton.

Clifford John Purnell

Charles Dando is recognised as the founder of the printing business in 1839, even though his occupation is given in the census returns as a Coal Agent. It is highly probable that his elder sister, Maria Dando Purnell marrying a printer and bookbinder, Charles John Hewitt, in 1839, and who lived in the Pithay in Paulton stimulated his interest in print.

Charles's eldest son Arthur ran the Midsomer Norton stationery shop and son Willie ran the Radstock shop, which also had a small printing shop. Both these shops closed as Purnells concentrated the business at Paulton in the 1920's.

Clifford Purnell was a devote and active Methodist, a life time bachelor, a non-smoker and a teetotaller. He was very upset at the hardship endured in Paulton following the closure of Flook's boot factory, due to the massive job losses and he vowed to expand the printing business to offer jobs to the unemployed. This promise was eventually fulfilled with the help of Wilfred Harvey.

The 1853 ledger of the firm, which has fortunately survived, gives a picture of the type of work undertaken and: following is a random selection of entries:

Folio 30   Mr Ferbrache. To print 20 bills of one guinea reward for names of persons throwing stones through the bedroom windows of Mr Firbanks.

Folio 31   Rev. C. C. Mayne
To printing 100 bills for Rev. Mayne notice of meeting of theBritish and Foreign Bible Society in Midsomer Norton.

Folio 32   Representatives of J. W. Rees-Moggs
100 bills £10 reward for conviction of persons stealing a stock lamb. Property of Mr Moses Higgs.

Folio 48   John Hill Esq. Paulton
100 bills of £10 reward for stealing a sheep from B Nash Esq. Ston Easton
1855
Folio 54   To 50 bills notice of a tea meeting   Rev. Stembridge

Folio 65   Lists of persons entitled to vote in the election of Knights of the Shire for the Eastern Division of the County of Somerset.

Folio 85   25 bills notice of Volunteer Rifle Committee Meeting at Chewton. 100 circulars for same. Mr John Parfit of Chewton.

Folio 86   Bills of notice for shooting match at Farrington Inn.

Folio 91   £10 reward: stealing potatoes at Blackfield Farm.

Folio 93   100 sheets showing the distance of coal carried on the Great Western Railway and rate for carriage.

Folio 101   Notice of Lecture on Colliery Accidents.

Folio 102   £1 reward on conviction of persons stealing four sides of bacon from Mr. Moses Parker.

Folio 103   £20 reward on conviction of persons for poisoning three dogs property of Mr Langford.

Folio 104   65 circulars to consider the expediency of forming a School Masters Association.

1856

Folio 105   25 bills of notice of collection on Thanksgiving Day in aid of the fund for a Memorial to Miss Nightingale.

Folio 106   To binding four volumes Illustrated London News in cases.

Folio 124   Mr.G. Carter, Paulton Inn 150 common sized cards for Ploughing Match, also Steeple Chase.

Folio 129   200 Crown Bills; sale of brewing plant, furniture, etc. at Bird-in-Hand Tavern, Pensford. Property of Mr. Hodges.

Folio 151   Railway Committee. Fear-Evans-Hill
To printing 50 prospectuses for proposed Mineral Railway with lithographed plans and schedule attached…………..£2-10-0

Folio 135   G. Carter, Paulton Inn To printing 250 cards "Journey's of Lloyd George"
50 crown bills Inspection of Rifle Corps.

1860

Folio 276   To print 200 summonses for witnesses in care of Bastard Children with Barstardy Summons for a witness on back.

Folio 303   Mr. H. Milward 50 Quarto bills notice of a meeting to consider the subject of the supply of gas in the Parish, also Penny Bank.

1861

Folio 304   Hymns for opening of New Coal Workings.

Quite a few railway schemes were proposed in the decade 1852-62 and C.D.Purnell & Sons printed most of the notices of meetings and prospectuses. Recorded in Folio 426 in September 1862 is an entry for the Bristol and North Somerset Railway Co. for printing the following:-

60 Extra Post circulars to School Masters to send in children to attend the ceremony of turning the First Sod at Clutton for the Bristol to Radstock line on 7th. October 1863.

120 Yellow cards for children	£1-6-0
3000 White cards for colliers	£3-0-0
3000 Cards for one pint and one quart	£1-16-6
200 Yellow cards for shareholders	£0-5-0
200 White cards for shareholders	£0-4-0
100 Programmes for schools	£0-7-0
1000 Bills directions colliers	£2-10-0
4000 Hymns on Superprint Post Paper	£3-5-6
3 Sheets Large Type 'Timsbury'	£0-1-6
'Camerton'	£0-1-6
'Clandown'	£0-1-6
'Radstock'	£0-1-6
'Norton Hill`	£0-1-6
'Old Welton'	£0-1-6
'William Hill'	£0-1-6
'Farrington Gurney'	£0-1-6
'Bishop Sutton'	£0-1-6
'Fry's Bottom'	£0-1-6
'Greyfields'	£0-1-6
6 Sheets Visitors Entrance	£0-2-6
2 Green Tickets Entrance	£0-1-6
6 Shareholders Entrance	£0-2-0
6 Colliers Entrance	£0-2-0
6 School Children`s Entrance	£0-2-0
40 To the Field	£0-5-0

It is interesting to note that this particular stretch of railway did not open until the 3rd September 1873, due to financial problems.

C. D. Purnell continued doing business with the Bristol and North Somerset for many years; Folio 444 dated 10th December 1864 records a sale of: -

$$3 \text{ boxes of wax tapers} \ldots\ldots\ldots\ldots \quad £0\text{-}4\text{-}6$$
$$200 \text{ quill pens} \ldots\ldots\ldots\ldots\ldots\ldots£1\text{-}0\text{-}0$$
$$500 \text{ foolscap envelopes} \quad \ldots\ldots\ldots £0\text{-}10\text{-}6$$

These items were sold through the stationery shop at High Park Corner.

The printing works, behind the shop at High Park Corner, where it had relocated sometime between 1851 and 1861, from the Pithay, had developed in size to such an extent that lack of space became a major problem. The garden of the premises had already been built over to house increasing production facilities such as type racks, composing frames, page and forme make-up benches and printing presses.

The land across the Hallatrow Road belonged to the Manor Farm Estate and was subject to an entail, which, for the time being, prevented it from being sold.

The presses employed at this time were three hand presses and one Cropper platen and all composing was done by hand.

In 1885 Charles Dando Purnell, now 62 years old, handed over the day-to-day management of the factory to his youngest son Clifford John Purnell, aged 20 years old.

It has been said that Clifford encouraged his father to take frequent holidays, a few days at Western- super- Mare, a few days elsewhere and every time he returned, young Clifford had rearranged this or moved something else in an effort to make better use of space.

It was Clifford that persuaded his neighbour, Mr. Styles, to allow him to build over his garden and then rent it back. There was one piece of land opposite High Park Corner, called The Pound, belonging to Joseph Flook (A descendant of the boot manufacturing family but now trading as a currier and grocer) and Charles Dando Purnell took out a mortgage on this land on 27th.February 1902. A pound was a piece of enclosed land where stray animals could be put until their owners could claim them; most large villages had them. The conveyance of land, including The Pound, from Charles Dando Purnell to his son Clifford took place on May 2nd. 1910.

In 1902 branches of Purnells were opened at Midsomer Norton and at Radstock. Clifford's eldest brother Arthur ran the Midsomer Norton stationers business situated in the Island and Willie Purnell ran the Radstock business.

A 1912 photograph of the Midsomer Norton branch of Purnell & Sons' shop in the Island.

The Midsomer Norton shop ran for many years and continued as a stationery shop long after Arthur Purnell moved out at the time when Purnells concentrated their three businesses at Paulton in the 1920's, getting out of the retail stationery side and focusing on book printing. Purnells also published and printed their own Almanac each year, which sold for a penny in 1903.

Meanwhile, space at Paulton was getting short again and Clifford Purnell was using his ingenuity by building upwards at the Park Corner site. Compare the photograph on page 13 to the earlier one on page two. The roof on the fourth building from the left has altered.

A 1912 photograph of the Radstock branch of Purnell & Sons, (extreme right) there was a small printing office as well as a shop here.

At Paulton, a gas engine to drive transmission belts for the presses had been installed and stop-cylinder type presses put into use; a Monotype keyboard and caster were bought in 1911 and stereotype equipment installed.

Charles Dando Purnell died in 1913, aged 91 years, peacefully and confident that he had left the business in very the capable hands of Clifford John Purnell his youngest son, who was keen to expand the business and get more involved with book work. However, book production requires a lot of specialised machinery particularly with the book binding operations, so, initially a decision was made to just compose and print the sheets and then send them out to trade book binders.

The most frequently used of these trade binders were, Webb Son and Co Ltd., The Ship Binding Works, Nevet Bookbinding Co. Ltd. and Key and Whiting, all in London.

By 1917 the number of Monotype keyboards and casters had increased to five, but the First World War was still raging and progress was slowed down; when the War finished in 1918 Clifford Purnell was one of the first to hear this news, as he had one of the first telephones in Paulton, and he promptly celebrated the event by hanging a Union Jack from his bedroom window.

The printing of bills, notifying people about forthcoming meetings etc, led to an addition to this business in the 1800's, that was pasting the bills up on rented hoardings in the surrounding district. This activity, known as Bill Posting, created the name Posters, and was only discontinued in1914 by Purnells. In 1855, the Rev. C.C. Mayne was charged 8/- for printing 100 Bills and 3/9 for posting them up.

Yet another line of the business was the production of picture postcards and many of Purnells postcards have been reproduced in books on the local history of the area. The ones with the titling, in white, sloping backwards, are the most easily recognisable.
The letter postcard, with a half penny stamp printed in one corner, was introduced in1870 but it took until 1899 before the reverse side might be used for a picture or advertisement. Picture Postcard collecting became a craze and by 1904, 16,000,000 weekly were being handled nationally by the Post Office.

Purnells had their own three, local outlets to sell the postcards in Radstock, Midsomer Norton and Paulton. Pictures of the local collieries, village views and, more sadly, mine disasters, featured on the postcards and form a very important element of the history of the area that embraces the Somerset Coal Field and the local railway halts and stations.

The Midsomer Norton mine disaster of 1908 was commemorated by a photograph, on a postcard and an example is shown later in this chapter.

The postcard is hand coloured, a practice used throughout the country at this time in the postcard business.

It is probable that the booming postcard business was responsible for the Radstock and Midsomer Norton branches opening up in 1902.

The Park Corner Composing Room in 1912. The comps are hand setting at the frames, the upper and lower cases in use; a term centuries old, but still in use today. Although the composing room looks well illuminated in daylight, the two gas batwing, type burners, seen over the frames, must have made evening work a great strain on the eyes.

Another 1920's photograph showing, on the right, the first buildings to be built on the land opposite Park Corner, Paulton.

A photograph of the first Monotype keyboard bought by the firm in 1911. The operator is thought to be Herbert Clements (joined 1903, retired 1946). Note the layout cards hanging on the window frame and an early copy of the Monotype Recorder on the window ledge.

The Monotype Caster bought in 1911, and installed in Park Corner, Paulton. The operators are thought to be Fred Symonds on the left and Jim Savery on the right. Notice the spirit burner that melted the type metal and the overhead drive belts.

A 1912 photograph of the pressroom in Park Corner, Paulton. The presses are belt driven and are of the stop-cylinder variety. The press on the left is printing a poster concerning Norton House.

One of the most important events to take place, locally, in 1914, was the lifting of the entail on the Paulton Manor Estate by the death of Colonel Molyneux Carter. There were 53 lots to be sold and of these 17 had changed hands by private treaty before the auction of the remainder in December 1914.

The Auctioneers were Messrs. Mabbett and Edge in conjunction with Mr. Thomas Melhuish. Included in the 17 lots dealt with by private treaty was the Red Lion Hotel, Paulton, which had been secured by Messrs. Coombe's Breweries Ltd.

The Manor Farm was lot No.12, extending to 104a 3r 11p, in the occupation of Mr. H.Hill. The bidding started at £4,000 and was subsequently purchased by Mr. Francis Pottecary, auctioneer of Andover for £5,000. The Manor Farm was now in the possession of Mr. Arthur Styles, Clifford Purnell's neighbour.

The binding department in 1912 at Park Corner. Nearly every operation is manual, although in the background can be seen some overhead shafting. Clifford Purnell can be seen on the extreme right overseeing the bindery operatives.

On May 20th 1919,Clifford Purnell bought from his neighbour, Mr. Arthur Styles, a piece of land measuring 105 ft. on the north side, 115 ft. on the south side and 64ft. on the east and west sides; this was part of Pigeon Close and was immediately to the west of the land purchased in 1902, fronting the Hallatrow Road. On this land was built, with direct labour, a building measuring 80ft. on the south and north sides and 60ft. on the east and west sides.

Two "Derriey" presses, French made and bought from Waterlows that could print both sides of the sheets in one pass through the press, were installed in this building. Both these presses were 8 Crown in size and joined a Quad Crown single "Derriey" press, an 8 Crown "Miehle", a Wharfedale and a Babcock.

The Purnell printers had difficulty in operating the French presses and a press minder from London, called Jack Cox was engaged together with his son Harold Cox and grandson Gordon Cox to operate these presses.

The type of work being undertaken at this time was more of a commercial nature, such as railway timetables and catalogues but Clifford Purnell still wanted to get into printing books.

Clifford Purnell met for the first time on January 1st. 1919 a young accountant aged 22 years old who worked for the firm of Curtis, Jenkins, Cornwell & Co. as an auditor, his name was Wilfred Harvey who had come to do the annual audit.

Wilfred Harvey visited every subsequent year to audit the accounts and Clifford Purnell was impressed by his interest in the industry generally. It must be pointed out that Wilfred Harvey, being based in Bristol, was auditing other printers and associated businesses such as Albert Pole and Sons Ltd. and Bristol Photo Engraving Ltd.

In the meantime a Mr. A.F. Waine was engaged as a Traveller, mainly for the London area, to visit publishers, take orders, and to keep the printing presses at Paulton busy

The first order obtained for a cased book, composing and printing only, was obtained from the publisher Herbert Jenkins in 1922 and was called "Shifting Sands" by Mrs. Patrick MacGill. The printed sheets were duly sent to London to a trade book binder.
  It was not until 1928 that a cased book was completely produced at Paulton and that again came from Herbert Jenkins and was titled "Young Entry".
  There was no London Sales Office at this time so Mr. Waine travelled to Town on the train from Hallatrow via Bristol and often stayed overnight in one of the numerous Commercial Hotels.

Here is a letter written by Mr. Waine on the 12th. May 1924 on hotel stationery, the Manchester Hotel in Aldersgate Street, London, E.C.1.

Dear Sirs,

As wired, you have apparently made a pretty fine mess of "Land of Lorna Doone". Mr. White sent for me and said, "You have lost all your laurels! This in one week - this and the Painted Honeymoon". Paragraph at end as deleted was so deleted in copy. Please look it up.

Print 7,000 4pp cancels.

Ring him up in the morning early – it is no good ringing me as I shall be going out at 9.00 a.m. or before. Match the paper. If you cannot – ring him through and he will get some on a passenger train.

In any case ring him up and explain. It may be that all is not deleted as I have marked, but follow copy.

I sincerely hope that we are not to blame. It has turned very hot and it's no joke to jog about in a heavy coat – sweating like a bull and a 'bully-ragging` at the end of it.

A.F.Waine

Mr. White was the General Manager of the publishing company Sampson Low and Marston Ltd., a company that Purnell was to do business with for many years. Eventually the company was entirely owned by Purnells, but more of this later.

It is evident from the foregoing, that the change from commercial printing work, to bookwork, was not an easy change and proof reading for bookwork had to be strengthened.

During one of several discussions that I had with Mr. Wilfred Harvey in the 1970`s, he informed me that he was asked by his company, at the suggestion of the Westminster Bank, to assist Clifford Purnell, in 1924, to help manage the rapidly growing business. I was told that he was appointed as Chief Accountant, but was never formally employed by Clifford Purnell, ever. Before he accepted however, Wilfred Harvey related that he took his wife out to Paulton and asked her "Well darling here it is, shall I have a go at it?" and his wife May's reply was "Well if anyone can do it, you can". Thus began an association, which saw an incredible growth in the firm of Purnell and Sons over the next 40 years.

The Manor Farm, acquired by Mr. Styles in 1914, still continued for a while as a farm. Purnell's bought extra land as and when they had the capital to do so.

On the 19th May 1924 two more pieces of land were purchased from Mr. Styles. The first piece measured 97ft. 6ins. on the north side and105 ft. on the south side, the east and west measured respectively 45ft. 3ins. and was situated immediately to the north and adjoining the first plot acquired in 1919.

The second piece of the 1924 purchase, measured 23ft. on the north and south sides and 107ft. 6ins. on the east and west sides. This plot adjoined the first plot on the west side. Into this building was installed an Eight Crown Huber press and a Quad Crown Dawson perfecting press.

The rear pressroom in 1912, showing a hand press in use and a Cropper platen. This is situated in the Park Corner premises, the belt shafting is a continuation of that shown in the picture on page 14.

A 1920's picture of the Manor Farm taken from the roof of the print works pictured below. The Monotype department was in the buildings to the right.

This picture was taken from a spot shown centre left in the photo above, in the 1920's and shows the Colour room in the left background, the Bindery and Press Rooms to the right.

In the upper picture, in the left background, can be seen Butlers Boot Factory that was soon to close in 1928, creating a lot of unemployment.

An aerial view of the new building programme taking place at the Manor Farm in The early 1930's. The lean-to building at the extreme left housed the folding room, which, together with the colour room and sewing room, was burnt in the 1941 fire. The stonewall seen at the extreme left of the photograph, leading to what was once Gate No. 4 of the factory, became the southerly wall of the covered way, known to all, as Temple-Meads. The boot factory, once owned by the Flook and Butler families, seen at the top left, is now a residential housing estate.

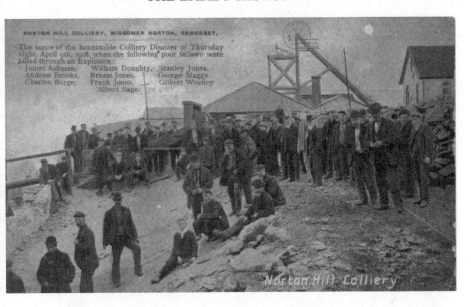

NORTON HILL COLLIERY, MIDSOMER NORTON, SOMERSET.

The scene of the lamentable Colliery Disaster of Thursday night, April 9th, 1908, when the following poor fellows were killed through an Explosion:

James Ashman,   William Doughty,   Stanley Jones,
Andrew Brooks,   Ernest Jones,   George Maggs
Charles Burge,   Frank Jones,   Gilbert Winsley
Albert Sage.

Norton Hill Colliery

The above card was hand tinted after printing.

POST CARD.

THIS SPACE FOR CORRESPONDENCE.   THE ADDRESS ONLY HERE.

INLAND POSTAGE ½d. FOREIGN POSTAGE 1d.

NORTON HILL COLLIERY, MIDSOMER NORTON, SOMERSET.

On Thursday night, April 9th, 1908, this pit was the scene of a calamity which filled the district with sorrow and horror.

Between 9 and 10 o'clock when the " Night Shift" had been down about an hour, it is supposed that the coal dust was ignited by blasting, and ten of the workers were added to the roll of victims of Colliery disasters, most of them being literally hurled into eternity, others having apparently succumbed to afterdamp. It was an unspeakable mercy that the explosion did not happen during the day when so many more men would have been in the mine, with relatively more terrible results.

The gloom, is lighted by the knowledge of the heroism displayed by the rescuers who nobly hastened to the work of rescue, and had in several cases to be themselves saved, their fellow helpers finding them insensible in the workings.

Dr. Pollard and Dr. Miall both descended the Shaft and rendered all possible assistance.

LIST OF KILLED:

James Ashman   William Doughty   Stanley Jones
Andrew Brooks   Ernest Jones   George Maggs
Charles Burge   Frank Jones   Gilbert Winsley
Albert Sage

Purnell & Sons, Paulton, Westwood & Midsomer Norton.

An example of a postcard produced by Purnells, just after the mining disaster at Midsomer Norton in 1908.

Purnell & Sons,

PAULTON, RADSTOCK,

AND

MIDSOMER NORTON,

Will be glad to receive your enquiries for

Printing,
Stationery,
Book=selling AND
Book=binding,

Of every description.

Private Posting Stations

Throughout the District.

Terms and List on application. . . . . .

Purnell

AND Sons,

PAULTON,
RADSTOCK
AND
MIDSOMER
NORTON.

An advertisement taken from the 1903 edition of the "Purnells' Illustrated Almanack" which sold for one penny.

CHAPTER TWO

THE ARRIVAL OF WILFRED HARVEY

Wilfred Harvey spent his time from 1924, learning all the aspects of typesetting, casting off copy, folding impositions, proofing, paper and press machining, as well as keeping the firm's accounts in order. No cased book binding was undertaken at Purnell; the sheets were sent out, mainly to London trade houses, and Clifford Purnell and Wilfred Harvey soon began to make plans to do all manufacturing in house, at Paulton. Their objective was as ever, to concentrate on books.

More Monotype keyboards and casters were added and the problem of low sales volume, addressed by renting St. Paul's Chambers, 19 Ludgate Hill, London, EC4 for £29-9-2 per quarter, in 1927. In addition office furniture amounting to £63-5-6 was installed. Mr A. F. Wain now had a London base, and to assist him, the cousin of Clifford Purnell, John Clifford Gibbs was engaged.

John Clifford Gibbs was born on the 10th. of March 1902 in Kent and was educated at Queens College, Taunton, a Methodist School. His first job was in the Coal Exchange, he was now 25 years old and had already played rugby in England's first 15 against Wales in 1925. He also played for England against New Zealand again in1925, against France in 1926, and against Scotland, Ireland, Wales and France in 1927, his home club was Harlequins, which he had joined in1918.

The England rugby team in 1927, at Twickenham, England v Wales. England won by 11 points to 9. Clifford Gibbs is the third player from the right, in the back row. Gibbs was thought by many to be the fastest wing three quarter ever to play for England.

Clifford Gibbs obtained a substantial order for the company, from the Wesleyan Methodist Missionary Society, on the 3rd. November 1927, entitled " Woman's Work".

A postcard was sent to Paulton from the London sales office as follows: -

Dear Harvey,

WESLEYAN METHODIST MISSIONARY SOCIETY
WOMANS WORK MAGAZINE

I have just heard over the `phone that we have secured this order. They are giving their present printers what they consider proper notice, viz: - three months; this means that we shall start with their March issue. I will send you further particulars tomorrow when I receive their official letter. This is good news for me.

J C Gibbs

The following day Mr A.F. Wain sent the following postcard: -

Dear Harvey,

WESLEYAN METHODIST MISSIONARY SOCIETY
Woman's Work Magazine

I am very pleased to hear that Gibbs was successful in getting the Magazines for the Wesleyan Methodist Society and as this is on your own costing it ought to be satisfactory. It is a nice little lump and I believe runs into about 7 or £800 a year.

Yours sincerely

A F Wain

It was the fashion at the time, for business colleagues to formally address each other by their surnames.

Mr. Wain left the firm shortly afterwards to join Ebenezer Baylis in Worcester. Mr Gibbs was left on his own for a while, until joined by Mr J. Murray Thompson, who later also became a director of Purnells.

At Paulton, the handling of the firm's finances, under Wilfred Harvey's guidance, during the period from 1925 to 1934, was under very tight control. To achieve the objective of binding the printed sheets at Paulton, a lot of varied and expensive machinery had to be acquired, to this end, payment by instalments was resorted to with the machinery suppliers. The Hire Purchase account for the period 1925 to1934 itemises the following purchases: -

April 5th.	1925 Two Quad Miehles, a 3 and a 4/0	Folio 30
Nov. 31st.	1925 1 x Furnival 8 Crown perfector	Folio 5
Nov. 25th.	1926 1 x 8 Crown perfector	Folio 25
Mar. 15th.	1926 1 x 8 Crown single	Folio 10
Dec. 17th.	1927 1 x Vertical Miehle	Folio 34
Mar. 27th.	1928 3 x Vertical Miehles	Folio 34
Mar. 31st.	1928 Furnival 40 x 60 press	Folio 34
May. 11th.	1928 Smyth-Horne	Folio 36
Sept.. 9th..	1928 Bookbinding Press	Folio 36

Mar. 9th.	1929 Baling Machine	Folio 36
Mar. 31st.	1929 Miehle perfector	Folio 15
May. 25th.	1929 Section Bundling Machine	Folio 37
May. 25th.	1929 Brehmer Sewing Machine	Folio 37
May. 25th.	1929 Tipping Machine	Folio 37
Sept. 10th.	1929 Murray 1st. and 2nd. Liner	Folio151
Nov. 20th.	1929 Friedheim Scoring Machine	Folio 150
Nov. 20th	1929 Beatrice Gold Blocking Machine	Folio 150
Nov. 20th	1929 2 x Book Sewing Machines	Folio 150
Dec. 15th.	1929 Section Bundling Machine	Folio 150
Jan. 12th.	1930 2 x Brehmer Sewing Machines	Folio 150
Feb. 14th	1930 2nd. Beatrice Case Blocker	Folio 150
Jan. 25th.	1932 2nd Guillotine	Folio 98
Mar. 4th.	1932 Babcock Drum Cylinder Press: Royal	Folio 98
May. 30th	1932 Brehmer Wire Stitcher	Folio 98
Sept. 9th.	1932 Monotype Keyboard and Caster	Folio 117
Nov 21st.	1932 Camco Folding Machine and Feeder	Folio 117
Dec. 7th.	1933 Sheridan Case maker	Folio 2
Dec. 7th.	1933 Knife Grinding Machine	Folio 152
Dec. 7th	1933 Smyth-Horne Casing-in Machine	Folio 152

The purchase of the three Vertical Miehle presses now meant that illustrations, and book jackets could now be printed in three colours, in house. Mr.Gibbs obtained the firms first colour order, which was a colour leaflet, advertising the book "Gentlemen Prefer Blondes"

It will be noticed that the cost of running the business was rising; extra machines meant extra wages, overheads and material costs. Getting the money owed, in quick enough, to pay the weekly wages and the repayments on the machinery, was a major problem. Mr. Gibbs told me that Wilfred Harvey was always chasing him to see customers who were behind with their accounts, to get cheques put on a passenger train at Paddington Station or Bills of Credit if the customer also had cash flow problems, sometimes as late as Thursday evenings in order to meet the wages due on Friday! Mr. Gibbs related that this went on for years as the firm expanded.

The Paulton factory, as it grew, obviously became more difficult to manage, and Clifford Purnell agreed to Wilfred Harvey's brother joining the firm in 1928. Wilfred Harvey by now was no longer just the accountant, but was managing the business also, with tight financial control.

William Frederick Harvey, (always known as Fred), came up from Crediton in Devon with his wife, sons Charles, Maurice and daughter Judith and spent the next 30 years as Works Manager and Works Director of Purnells.

Most of the early building, done by direct labour, was constructed of local stone, with wooden, tarred, felt roofs; on the 19th.September 1924 Austin Bourton who was engaged on this work, as a mason's labourer, fell 30 ft. from a ladder and badly injured himself, Clifford Purnell rushed him to Paulton Hospital in his car. In fact, this was a bad week for accidents at the factory because Mr. Bill Draper, a machine engineer, got his head caught between the buffer piston and buffer cylinder on a two-revolution printing press. He sustained a fractured nose and severe head injuries; luckily the local doctor, Dr. Miall, was on hand to take him to Paulton Hospital. Mr. Draper became the factory's Chief Engineer and eventually a Director of the firm.

Conditions in the locality were harsh during these years; in 1928 the local Butler Boot factory closed down after trading for 25 years and put many men out of work.

Clifford Purnell often said that he recalled the closure of the Flooks Boot factory in 1898, which caused terrible hardship in Paulton, and resolved to do the best he could to give employment to as many as possible.

The need for capital, to purchase machinery, from the second half of the 1920's made Wilfred Harvey and Clifford Purnell approach members of the staff for cash loans; the response was good. The Loans Raised Folio, for the period 31st. Mar 1926 to Oct 1932 records the following Paulton staff making loans, but excludes the London Office staff who also made loans: -

1926 Mar 31st.	W.Harvey	£125-0-0
1927 Aug	John Richards Uren Brooks	£70-0-0
	Frank Howard	£100-0-0
	Albert Edward Fear	£100-0-0
	Henry Herbert Clements	£400-0-0
	P. Jones	£6-0-0
	William Horace Draper	£100-0-0
	William John Carter	£110-0-0
Sept.	John Grenville Pounds	£150-0-0
	George Herbert Fricker	£150-0-0
Oct	George Herbert Fricker	£200-0-0
	W. Harvey	£200-0-0
	J. R. U. Brooks	£16-0-0
1928 Jan	G. H. Fricker	£50-0-0
Feb	J. R. U. Brooks	£10-0-0
Mar	J. R. U. Brooks	£20-0-0
	William John Carter	£40-0-0 J.
	R. U. Brooks	£10-0-0
	Percy Jones	£5-0-0
Jul	J. R. U. Brooks	£10-0-0
Aug	J. R. U. Brooks	£7-0-0
Oct	J. R. U. Brooks	£15-0-0
Nov	W. F. Harvey	£75-0-0
	W. H. Draper	£100-0-0
1929 Aug	W. H. Draper (12 months)	£200-0-0
	W. J. Carter (12 months)	£100-0-0
	Frank Howard (12 months)	£150-0-0
	H. Clements (12 months)	£50-0-0
	J. R. U. Brooks (12 months)	£50- 0-0-
Nov	W. H. Harvey	£48- 0-0
	W. H. Harvey	£15- 0-0
	W. H. Harvey	£63- 0-0
1930 Aug	W. J. Carter	£30- 0-0
	J. R. U. Brooks	£102-14-0

By 1932 the unsecured loans of the employees totalled £7,512-17-3

The sundry loans totalled	£4,366-15-0
The loans on mortgage were	£2,250-0-0

It was frequently said, in future years, that these employee loans were repaid handsomely. In October 1932, the cash flow problem caused Wilfred Harvey to write to staff and reduce their wages to improve the situation.

Building of production and storage departments continued at Paulton at an increasing pace during the early 1930`s. It should be noted that the production of books, unlike commercial print work, at this period in time, required vast amounts of storage space. Publishers would expect printers to keep the type matter, or stereo plates of titles, for long periods so that reprints could be quickly achieved, furthermore, they would place print orders far in excess of the binding orders, on titles that they were confident of selling well. The printer was expected to store these extra printed sheets, rent free, for months and sometimes years. Some printers also undertook the storage and distribution of the bound books.

Clifford Purnell bought the Manor Farm from Mr. Styles on the 24th. March 1930; this added 24.975 acres to his existing holding of land on the North side of Hallatrow Road. Further purchases were made, for example on the 29th.December 1932, 39 perches and 22 square yards of land was bought, again from Mr.Styles, adjoining the Pigeon Close building. Part of the old Butler Boot Factory was bought, back on 27th. January 1928 from William Freshwater. A piece of land, being a garden and paddock, near the Red Lion public house, was bought from the Oakhill Breweries on the 23rd. August 1934, and on the 25th.October 1933 Clifford Purnell had bought a piece of land, part of Wall Close Orchard, with a factory and building from Walter James Edwards.

This holding of land represented the entire land held by Clifford Purnell in 1935 when he sold it to the company to form Purnell and Sons Ltd. The company acquired much more land after 1935.

The customer list in the early 1930`s was quite impressive and reflected the hard work that Mr. Gibbs and his sales team had put in, closely monitored by Wilfred Harvey. Regular work was being carried out for the following customers: -

Army and Navy Stores (Catalogue), Methodist Missionary Society, A. C. Black Ltd., Methuen and Co.Ltd., George Newnes Ltd., Ivor Nicholson and Watson Ltd., George Bell and Sons Ltd., Oxford University Press, Children's Special Service Mission, C. Arthur Pearson Ltd., Dean and Sons Ltd., Sampson Low Marston and Co. Ltd., George G. Harrap and Co. Ltd., Frederick Warne and Co. Ltd., Herbert Jenkins Ltd., Macmillan and Co. Ltd. and Marshall, Morgan and Scott, Ltd.

Wilfred Harvey reckoned that the factory had, in terms of size and capacity, increased by eight times, from 1924 to1934. It was becoming so successful that work was being turned away due to insufficient capacity, and this rankled with Wilfred Harvey. With the acquisition of the Manor Farm in 1930, a massive building programme commenced in 1931 and 1932 on the newly bought land. At the same time more machinery was bought on Hire Purchase; all this being financed by loans and extended credit from suppliers. The need for capital now became so pressing that Clifford Purnell and Wilfred Harvey met Clifford Gibbs at Paddington Station and told him the position that it would be difficult to carry on the business without further capital. It was Clifford Gibbs who arranged a meeting with a solicitor friend who was in contact with the Banks and arranged for the Company to be "Held" until it became a Public Company in 1935. The Solicitor was Stafford Clark and Co., at 3 Laurence Pountney Hill, London, E.C. 4.

During Wilfred Harvey's dealings with machinery suppliers, he and Clifford Purnell made some useful contacts and friends, one of the most influential of these was Captain Roderick Horne, who was the European agent for the Smyth Manufacturing Company based in Hartford, USA. In fact, his London based company was called Smyth-Horne Ltd. The Smyth Company Co. made excellent book binding machinery that had a worldwide reputation for mechanical perfection and reliability. Roderick Horne also represented the Harris press company and the Cottrell press makers, again both based in the USA.

WILFRED HARVEY.

It was Roderick Horne who arranged Wilfred Harvey's first trip to the USA, the first of many; he was also one of the first to be confidentially informed of Purnell and Sons changing from a firm to a company, as early as the 29th. September 1934, after all, Purnells did owe him rather a lot of money. The correspondence between the two was voluminous, covering not only presses and bookbinding machines, but what books, especially children's books were selling in the American shops. Coloured children's books were of particular interest to Wilfred Harvey, literally in all shapes and sizes, later " Animal Cut Out Books" became a popular line for Purnells. These books, known as Toy Books, held Wilfred Harvey's attention for some time, they were mass produced in the USA, a typical example was "Mickey Mouse", which sold for 10 cents in 1933 through the Woolworth's stores. The Americans printed this type of work on Cottrell, four colour, sheet fed, rotary letterpress machines and Harris Offset Litho presses. Roderick Horne wrote to Wilfred Harvey on 23rd. March 1934: -

Confirming our telephone conversation this morning, I consider it very necessary for you folks to seriously consider this new Cottrell colour press as it is considered to produce colour work equally as good as you can get from the two revolution presses, but at far greater economy. These Cottrell, four colour, McKee sheeted rotaries have been on the American market for the last 25 years or so and there are an enormous number of them in use, many of the big magazine and general printers having rows of them in successful operation.
These colour presses have always been too big and too costly for the European market, but, at the request of the jobbing colour printers in the States, and I might also say ourselves over here, the Cottrell folks were persuaded to design and build a fast running, small size press, which will take a maximum sheet up to 35" x 47" and to run at a speed of 4,000-4,500 sheets hourly, printing 1 to 4 colours.
Dexter's new Pile Feeder is used which can even feed sheets up to 5,000 an hour, or more. There is one big impression cylinder, and only one set of grippers and the four plate cylinders bear on the big impression cylinder. Seeing that there is only one grip to the sheets, providing that the colour cylinders are adjusted to register before

starting, then one meets with no trouble with atmospheric conditions and the colours are always in perfect register one to the other, and where superimposing takes place, this is done of course, by one wet colour on another.

As regards making the curved plates and also most of the make-ready, this is done away from the press. I have been in touch with Mr.Cosey of Messrs. Nickeloids, London, and they are willing to make these Cottrell McKee plates and the make-ready providing they obtain the contract for at least a year after the press is running. I am sending you two sheets, both of which have passed through the big Cottrell four colour sheet fed press at a speed of 3,000 sheets per hour. Of course, please remember that we are talking about printing on one side only.

I would very much value what Mr. Purnell and you think of the quality of this wet on wet colour printing and its speed. A smaller press which I am bringing forward is to run at the high speed of 4,000-4,500 sheets per hour and I have today cabled to the Cottrell folks asking for their price, also time of shipment, and the press to be installed on a two months trial basis and subject to its performing its work in a suitable manner, then it would be accepted and paid for.

We would no doubt have to attach a wax sprayer this end, because the American wax sprayer is three times the price of ours.

Yours truly,

R.W.Horne

Following this particular correspondence, and several telephone conversations, on colour printing, letterpress rotary, and children's books in the USA, Roderick Horne wrote to Wilfred Harvey on the 28th.March 1934, as follows: -

Yesterday you will recall that we were talking about colour presses, and I brought to your attention the Harris two colour, sheet fed rotary press and I suggest that you give this press your serious consideration.

Mr. Roche, of the Harris-Seybold-Potter Company happens to be with us at the present time, and I was considerably surprised to hear from him that about three years ago the big and well known magazine printers located just outside New York City, The Conde Nast Co. asked the Harris folks to build them a sheet fed, two colour, rotary press to handle well known magazines as "Vanity Fair" and "Vogue", calling for high class black and colour printing.

The press was installed and it was so satisfactory that they ordered a further eleven and now they have twelve running and have disposed of 22 two-colour Miehle presses.

As I have told you, in the last few months, the tendency in America for the last three or four years has been in the direction of these two and four colour, sheet fed, rotary presses, taking the place of the flatbed, two revolution Miehles, simply because the quality of the printing is just as good as you can get from the Miehle, if not better, and the actual output is more than double, and thus there is sufficient economy to warrant Miehle presses being displaced by these new rotary presses.

The presses were of course, rotary, letterpress machines and not lithographic presses, but it did not take Roderick Horne long, to bring toWilfred Harvey's attention, that Harris also made very good litho-presses.

Mr.Boon, also from Smyth-Horne Ltd. visited Clifford Purnell and Wilfred Harvey in early September 1934, and reported back to his boss, Roderick Horne, that Purnells were investigating the possibility of using sheet fed lithographic presses for their books.

Roderick Horne quickly sent the following letter to Wilfred Harvey:-

September 19th. 1934
Mr.Boon has returned from paying you a visit, last week and he advises that you are seriously considering the use of offset presses and that you are wanting to have some idea of the capital outlay to start an offset printing department.
We are afraid that this is asking for a lot of information that we do not have, but we may be able to obtain from several suppliers of the plant necessary for making the offset zinc or aluminium plates, but would it not be possible for you to obtain these plates made outside by the

trade plate makers, thus enabling you to install, say one or two offset presses, and when you are familiar with the working of same and find it a success and wanting more offset presses, at the same time you could lay down a plate making department?

Of course when you are paying your visit to the States, which we hope will be in the near future, the Harris Potter folks would be only too pleased to give you all the information from the plate making plant to the cost of the presses.

We can give the latter right away.

R W Horne

Wilfred Harvey sent a letter to Roderick Horne on the 28th. September 1934: -

Between ourselves, we hope very shortly to form this firm into a company when your account will be dealt with immediately. I hope to have some definite news on this subject very shortly and I will communicate with you immediately.

Please treat this information as private and confidential.

Yours sincerely,

W. Harvey

To which Roderick Horne replied on October 1st. 1934: -

Your most interesting, newsy, letter of the 28th. Ultimo to hand this morning and you can rely upon my treating this information very confidentially.

I take it for granted that whatever new arrangements as regards the firm takes place, it will be to the advantage of both Mr. Purnell and yourself.

> *With best wishes*
> *Yours sincerely*

> *R W Horne*

WILFRED HARVEY.

There is no doubt that Roderick Horne's advice and help influenced many of Wilfred Harvey's decisions on the selection of presses and even the type of children's toy books that he was to become involved with in the near future. The Company bought a Cottrell four colour, sheet fed, letterpress rotary press, and eventually acquired a controlling interest in the company that made its plates, Nickeloid Ltd. Harris, two and four colour offset presses were bought and put into production, shortly after the Company had been floated.

However, letterpress was still, at this time, the major process with Linotype and Miehle Two Colour presses and Perfecting Presses still being dominant in most major book printing houses.

The firm of Purnell and Sons became Purnell and Sons Ltd. on the 25th.March 1935. The Share Capital was £250,000 split as £150,000 as150,000 6% Cumulative Preference Shares of £1 each, and 500,000 Ordinary Shares of 5s. each. The Preference Shares were valued at £125,000 and the Ordinary Shares at £125,000.

The Directors of the new company were: -
Clifford John Purnell, Park Corner, Paulton, near Bristol (Printer), Chairman.

Wilfred Harvey, Willington House, Midsomer Norton, near Bath (Printer)
Managing Director.

John Clifford Gibbs, 36 Hammelton Road, Bromley, Kent (Printer)
Sales Director.

Frank Alan Pratley, F,C,A., Sherwood, Beresford Road, Cheam, Surrey
(Partner in Davie Parsons and Co., Chartered Accountants).

The Secretary was Stanley Victor Wilshire and the Registered Office was The Works, Paulton, near Bristol.

It is interesting to note, that in the Prospectus, that the founding of the Company is given as 1849, but this probably refers to Charles Dando Purnell's fulltime involvement in the business, as we know that the 1841 Census shows, Charles Hewitt, his son in law, as a printer and bookbinder, so some sort of printing business was already at the Pithay, Paulton at that time.

The Prospectus also quotes parts of the Articles of Association, and gives the following Contracts, that had been entered into: -
19th. March 1935 between the Company of the one part and Wilfred Harvey of the other part, whereby the company appoints the said Wilfred Harvey as Managing Director for seven years at a salary at the rate of £1,250 per annum and a commission in respect of each financial year of 4 per cent. on the net profits up to £20,000, and of 5 per cent. on the net profits over £20,000, such net profits to be ascertained in the manner therein provided (such remuneration to include his fixed remuneration as an Ordinary Director).

19th. March 1935, between the company of the one part and John Clifford Gibbs of the other part whereby the Company appoints the said John Clifford Gibbs as Sales Director for seven years at a salary at the rate of £1,000 per annum (such remuneration to include his fixed remuneration as an Ordinary Director).

The Company now had Capital, and on the 8th. April 1936 a new subsidiary company called Paulton Holdings Ltd. was formed, the initial capital was £5,000. The purpose of the new company was to supply the parent company with orders, materials, equipment and allied processes. The Directors of this company were Clifford Purnell, Wilfred Harvey, John Clifford Gibbs and Frank Alan Pratley.

The first publishing company created by Purnells, as related to me by Clifford Gibbs, was not without problems. As Sales Director, Clifford Gibbs thought that existing customers would be driven away by having their printer in competition with them, but he had to concede the argument, and with the passage of time Wilfred Harvey was proved to be correct.

WILFRED HARVEY.

On the 27th.March 1936, Juvenile Productions Ltd, was incorporated, No.312222. This it will be noticed, was two weeks before Paulton Holdings Ltd. was incorporated.

Purnells were printing and binding a considerable amount of books in 1936 for Raphael Tuck and Sons Ltd., one of Clifford Gibbs accounts, the man responsible for children's books there was a Mr Stanley E. Jackson. Wilfred Harvey managed to get Stanley Jackson to organise and manage Juvenile Productions as a Director with E. J. Upperton as the second Director. The company's banner headline was "Book Publishers for Children of all Ages". They set up company in Ludgate House, 110-111 Fleet Street, London EC4.

Extraordinary General Meetings of Paulton Holdings took place to increase the Capital of the Company on the following dates:
23rd. September 1936, 10,000 £1 Shares, increasing the Capital to £15,000.
22nd. September 1937, 45,000 £1 Shares, increasing the Capital to £60,000.
27th. September 1939, 40,000 £1 Shares, increasing the Capital to £100,000.

Another company was created on the 17th July 1936 called Paper Novelties Ltd., the Registered number being 31651, the manufacturing being based at Paulton. This company was concerned with the manufacture of Christmas decorations such as garlands, bells, crackers, hats and general decorations. The Share Capital was £1,000 as 1,000 £1 Shares and the first Directors were, William Grigg and Edward James Upperton. The London Sales Office was 107 Fleet Street, London EC4. It is interesting to note that by August 1938 the Directors had increased to S E Jackson, W Grigg, E J Upperton and H Schlesinger, the latter felt it necessary to have the following printed after his name on the letter headings: (British formerly Austrian), no doubt a reflection of the political troubles in Europe at this time. By December 1938 Schlesinger's name had disappeared from the letter headings.

WILFRED HARVEY.

A complicated legal argument developed between the Company and Mr Grigg, over his claim to a patent for a new style Christmas cracker, called the Honeycomb Cracker. Apparently, Mr Schlesinger got a German firm to make a line garland machine, in the early days of the company. Mr Grigg, who made several visits to the Paulton factory, conceived an idea that a garland cracker could be made, or the foundation for it, on the garland machine. A provisional patent was placed in Mr Griggs name, as Purnells did not want the outside world to know of Purnells connection to Paper Novelties Ltd. Purnells had employed Mr Grigg since the 15th. February 1936 at a wage of £3 per week plus commission in getting sales. He became a Director later that year when the new company was incorporated. An agreement between the two was reached on the 27th. April 1938. Wilfred Harvey's brother, A J Harvey (Bert) came in to manage this department briefly until the out break of the second world war when he went on active service and the department eventually closed.

One of the main customers for Garlands (as it became known locally) was Dean and Co Ltd., this company sent orders all over the world. Littlewoods, Barlow and Parker, W H Smith Ltd. and many more were all disappointed when the department had to close in 1940.

On the 23rd.September 1940, Wilfred Harvey wrote to his customer friend, Mr Bradban at Dean and Sons Ltd.: -

Dear Mr Bradban,

In reply to your letter of the 19th. inst. regarding garlands I am sorry, I cannot offer you anything at the moment.
To be perfectly frank with you we have offered everything connected with this department, including plant, to a man who is interested to take over the lot.
I have decided to close down this department.

Yours sincerely
W. Harvey

At this stage there were eight girls working on garlands, two on box making, one boy box making, two boys on presses, one boy on packing, one office girl and one forewoman.

Purnells had already entered the publishing world with the formation of Juveniles back in March 1936, but another opportunity presented itself when Murray Thomson, in Purnell Sales had confidential talks with one of his customers during the spring of 1938. This customer was Theodore Macdonald, a director of Robert Hale and Company, publishers, based at 102 Great Russell Street, London WC1. Mr. Macdonald was the director mainly concerned with sales and production at Hales, but he was restless and wanted to start up in business on his own account, but he lacked the capital necessary to begin.

Murray Thompson related Mr. Macdonald's aspirations to his boss Clifford Gibbs and to Wilfred Harvey. This time, Clifford Gibbs fears about printers getting involved in publishing could lose them customers, was heeded by Wilfred Harvey, and he sent a teleprinter message to Murray Thomson from Paulton saying, "We would be prepared to finance Macdonald to the tune of £5,000 on the condition that no one knows of Purnells involvement in this enterprise and if any one asks, tell them that Purnell is helping Macdonald with credit on printing and binding".

On the 16th May 1938 Murray Thomson sent this letter to Wilfred Harvey:-

Dear Harvey,

MACDONALD.

Macdonald is giving Hale notice this morning.
He anticipates that he will make at least one wide journey over England, Scotland and Ireland on behalf of Hale before he leaves.
On this journey he will do full propaganda work for the new series.
Following at least a fortnight on full time for Hale he thinks it is possible that he will be nominally working for Hale for a further six weeks but with the understanding that he remains in London and is

free to do preparatory work on his own behalf. So far as possible during this period he will draw full pay from Hale, but I have told him that if he finds Hale sticky about this we shall make up to him what he loses from Hale.

While he is away from London he will keep me regularly posted as to his address. On his return we shall arrange to meet almost daily. He will lose no time in getting after titles and rights. We shall not get down to seeking offices until he is in London.

So far as stocking, delivery, invoicing and all accountancy are concerned I suggest that we should closely follow methods between Juveniles and yourselves and I see no objection to taking Macdonald to visit Juveniles to see what is done. It is probable that we can find a girl clerk who, for the present at any rate, can do all that is necessary.

Macdonald will concentrate on 3d`s and Demy 8vo. 6d`s. His selling experience makes him very emphatic that there is the demand for both these, especially the latter where there is little supply at present. He is very disinclined to add another "Penguin" to the great number already out.

I have strongly impressed on Macdonald that success depends on his own methods; that he can approach you freely on any point at any time – I have drawn strong comparisons between Hale and yourself in your methods of treating a subordinate. While encouraging him to feel very free to refer to you I have invited him to look on me as your representative in London. I am, as a matter of fact, looking forward to an interesting and happy time in learning something of the publishing trade. So far as the public is concerned the story will be that Macdonald found a little money and found Purnells willing to help him still further with credit, but that apart there is no connection between Purnells and the new firm.

Yours sincerely

J. M. Thomson

PS I shall see Jackson first to get all the office documentation and shall not be in a hurry to introduce Jackson to Macdonald but I see no objection to my doing this eventually.

CHAPTER THREE

THE EARLY 1930'S FACTORY LAYOUT

It can be seen from the photographs of the buildings exteriors, shown in the previous chapter, that there was not a lot of space available for the bulky business of producing books. Some of these buildings were also two floors high, again not ideal for efficient production.

A look inside these buildings, as they were in 1930-1933, will show the staff, the machines of that time and the general working conditions.

A photograph taken in November 1932 of the Stone Room in the Park Corner premises. In this picture can be seen Cliff Clarke, Fred Savage, John R. U. Brooks (Overseer), Stan Hunt, Herbert Clements, Wally Bridges, Colwin Shipley, Alfred Gillard, Victor Savage, David Flint, Jack Dutton, Roland Pickford, Roland Blisset, Jim Weeks, Fred Shearn, Bert Chivers, Charlie Lanning, Cecil Rogers, Reg Bennet, Fred Bartlet, George Woodburn, Les Mitchard, Horace Prew, Richmond Biss, Ken Hancock, Len Groves, J. Davis (Taffy), and Harry Pocock.

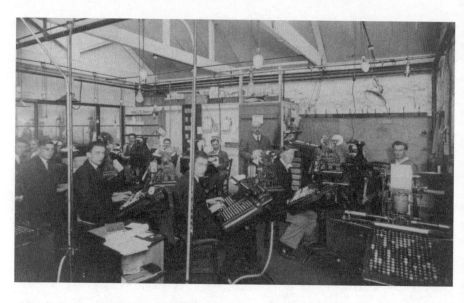

The Monotype Keyboard department in 1932. In this Picture are Jack Clements, John Pounds (Overseer), George Cook, Albert Burge, Harold Brooks, John Brice, Vic Bisgrove, Wilf Shearn, and Les Mitchard.

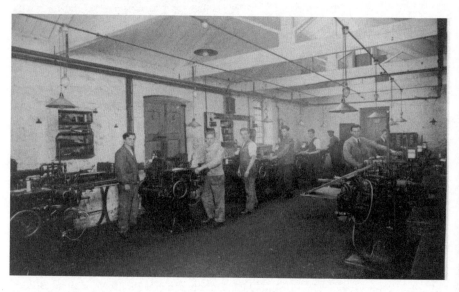

The Monotype Casters in 1932. The operators are Donovan Sherbourne, Roy Long, Raymond Davenport, George Banfield, Albert Shearn, Stanley Heal, Gerald Tidcombe.

The Stereo Plate Making Department, flong making in 1932. The operators are Harry Sayer and William Carter.

The Colour Room in 1932.Four Vertical Miehle presses working on book jackets. Pictured here are William Brooks, Bert Howe, Ken Janes and Stanley Evans.

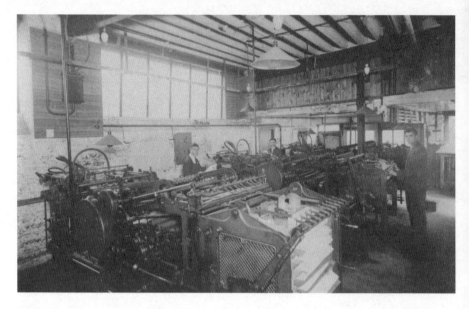

The Colour Room, three Horizontal Miehle presses in1932. The operators are Cliff Comer, Reg Fear and Fred Carter

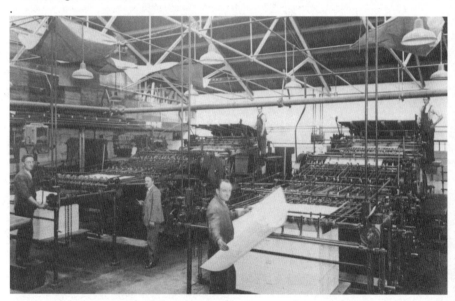

Two of the eight Quad Demy Perfecting Presses in 1932, with Cross Feeders and extended deliveries. In the picture are Tom Briers, James Savery (Overseer), Bill Parnell, Len Seaford and Percy Barnett.

This picture was taken from between the two presses in the previous picture. In both pictures can be seen sheets of paper suspended from the roof joists, there must have been a few roof leaks.

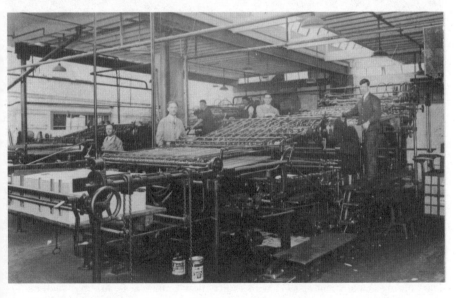

More Perfecting presses, with Len Tuck, Percy Jones, Maurice Parfit, Tom Evans, George Williams and Harry Bush. There are tins of Coates ink under the ink duct.

Another of the Perfectors with Fred Tranter and Cecil Wych on the press in 1932.

The Folding Department in 1932 with a fairly new Camco S. C. folding machine. The staff pictured is Fred Lockyear, Stan Webb (Foreman), Gwen Francis, Alwyn Elms, and Bert James.

Clifford Purnell's notes on the back of the original photograph, sings the praises of this particular machine, as follows:- " A wonderful folding machine, probably the most perfect folding machine in the world, and at present, the only one. This machine will take an 8Crn. sheet, fold eight sections of 16pp., auto collate and gather in correct order for sewing, at a rate of 2,500-3,000 8Crn. sheets per hour.

The Folding Department with Jack Woodland, Gladys Redwood, Doreen Perry, Betty Purnell, and Ivy Coughlin in 1932.

The lean-to building above, which housed the Folding Department, can be seen on the extreme left of the aerial photograph shown earlier.

The 1941 fire did extreme damage to the machines, but thankfully no one was injured in this incident.

In the series of photographs of the Bindery now following, one will see the same girls on different machines within the various sections of the Bindery; they did have to be multi-skilled to cope with the wide variety of operations. Furthermore, one suspects that they knew they were to have their pictures taken, they are all smartly dressed with neat hairstyles.

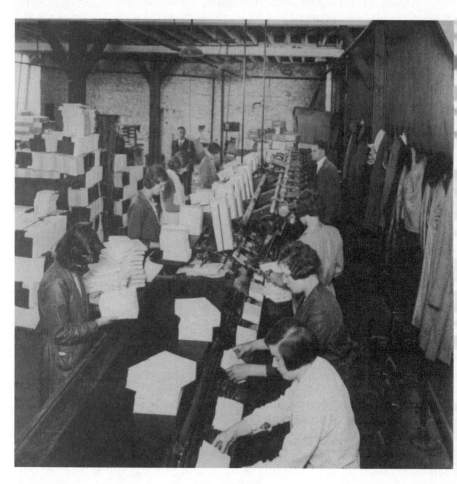

The Bindery in 1932, the Gathering and collating section working on a 10 station Jeungst Gathering machine. The girl in the left foreground is doing the collating. Shown in this picture is Emrys Whitton (Overseer), Ivy Dando, Stella Banfield, Hanna Derrick.

It should be noted in this chapter, that the head of the Monotype Keyboards, had a tragic, fatal accident, on his way to work one foggy morning, just before Christmas in 1934. John Greville Pounds, aged 52 years, was driving to work with a companion who worked at

Purnells', when they skidded into a bank at Marksbury, in very dense fog. They heard an approaching vehicle and Mr. Pounds stood in the road with his arms outstretched in an attempt to stop it.

Both were struck by the van and Mr. Pounds did not survive. He was also a well-known local organist.

The Tipping Machine, bought in 1929, seen attaching endpapers to first and last book sections. Hanna Derrick and Phyllis Church are pictured on the machine.

The Upper Bindery in 1932, showing girls tipping-in plates into sections, by hand and inserting. The girls shown are Joyce Box, Mildred Sims, Ivy Padden, Olive Jarvis, Olive Moon, Cissie Smith, Gwen Down and Netta Bull.

The book Sewing Room in 1932 showing a mixture of Smyth and Brehmer machines. In the picture are Ernest Endacott (Foreman), Netta Snelling, Phyllis Wych, Stella Banfield, Joyce Shearn, Winnie Weeks, Ivy Blake, Jessie Jenkins, Evelyn Minall, Ivy Padden, Phyllis Woodland, Sylvia Down, Olive Stevens, Nora Filer, Phyllis Norris, V. Hand, Vera Carter, Joyce Carter, and Joyce Box.

The Bindery with three Smyth wing type casing-in machines in operation. Pictured are Arthur Dredge, Alfred Goddard, Raymond Carter, Norman Wiltshire, Fred Tuck, Bert Webb and Mr. Plumley.

The Case making Department in1932. A Smyth No.2 Case maker being operated by Dick Truscott and Arthur Pain. The cases are being made from printed paper covers, the machine has an automatic feeder for the covers

Clifford Purnell, photographed in his car, in the late 1920's. This car was used on many occasions to transport employees who had been injured in accidents to Paulton hospital, including those that suffered on the cricket field at weekends.

Practically all of the machinery seen in the photographs, in this chapter, of the bindery, was obtained from Smyth-Horne Ltd., through various deals put together by Wilfred Harvey and Captain Roderick Horne, the European agent for the American bookbinding machine manufacturer Smyth. Their association extended beyond business and they became firm friends over many years, Roderick Horne stayed at Wilfred Harvey's home, The Chase at Winsley on several occasions.

CHAPTER FOUR

LIHOGRAPHY and the BUDWIGS

The introduction of lithography into Purnells is a very interesting story on its own.

Roderick Horne had already sent samples of four and two colour offset litho printing to Clifford Purnell and Wilfred Harvey from the USA, to compare with the colour letterpress work being produced at Paulton. The quality of the Harris presses was satisfactory, the output of printed sheets per hour was more than satisfactory; the problem lay with the provision of litho printing plates. The most sensible way out seemed to be the use of trade plate makers, but then Wilfred Harvey met a German gentleman called Dagobert Budwig.

Mr. Budwig was a Director of a large Berlin printing works who made frequent visits to Britain to obtain orders for his works. In 1936 Mr Budwig called on Mr Bradban the Managing Director of Dean and Sons Ltd. and was shown a "Mickey Mouse" sample book which was published in this country by Birn Bros. Now Wilfred Harvey knew Monty and Maurice Birn well, they were Jewish, and so was Mr Budwig who also knew the Birns. Purnells had printed the "Mickey Mouse" book for Birns and when Clifford Gibbs and Wilfred Harvey found out about this they were furious, because Wilfred Harvey had worked hard in introducing these new toy books to Deans and others from what he had seen in the USA. What Mr Bradban did not know was that Mr Budwig and Wilfred Harvey also knew each other from joint ventures they had investigated together such as the production of

"Magic Painting Books" This incident rankled with Wilfred Harvey for a long time.

The political situation in Germany was not easy for anyone of the Jewish faith in 1936 and was worsening day by day. Dagobert Budwig had a son Stephan who was a top authority on lithographic technical matters in Germany; Wilfred Harvey arranged to see both of the Budwigs in Bath on the 19th. April 1937 to discuss the creation of a Purnell lithographic plate making department and he had intimated to them that they might manage it.

Dagobert Budwig wrote to Wilfred Harvey on the 7th. April 1937: -

"Sorry that I have no reply from you to my last two letters referring to the paintless painting books and to my enquiry with reference to the Animal Cutout Books. There will probably be another chance to make a penny painting book. I think they should be made up differently to those that you have formerly printed in three colours on both sides. The customer wants these goods at 4/3 but they might possibly go up to 4/6 per gross for six designs of 1000 gross each. Please keep this information strictly confidential.

I have got the invitation from the passport control officer of the British Embassy in Berlin and have seen the gentleman in charge. I hope that he will send a favourable report to London. As you see these things are much more delayed as we both anticipated. Naturally, the delay also occurs on this side. Therefore I propose the following proceeding, if you do not advise me to the contrary.

I intend to be in your London office on the 16th. April and go to either the same day or the next day to Bath to find a suitable lodging. I could then be at your disposal entirely at Paulton on Monday the 19th. April and I Presume that also my son can sever his connection with me at the same day at Paulton.

I think it advisable to go to your factory over with you in order to find out which machinery could be used for the new department and at the same time to discuss which machinery would have specially to be bought for this department either from English sources or sources abroad. This proceeding may require my staying in Bath for a fortnight until all offers come in. After that time I would like to go back to Germany for a few days in order to assist my wife in the removal of our furniture, etc. then going back to England to take up permanent residence there. My son would naturally not go back with me to Germany and could remain in Paulton or Bath respectively. Should you take any objection to this proceeding, kindly send me a telegram "Delay departure".

In the meantime I hope to have an answer to my previous letter and I should also appreciate it if you would reply to my today's letter by airmail so that I could govern myself accordingly.

Our mutual friends do not know anything about my new plans as arranged with you, these should be kept secret until we both agree upon the date this information should be sent them.

I remain

With kind regards

D. Budwig

PS Your letter of the 5$^{th..}$ Inst. just to hand. Have you made the experiments with a rubber block and with aniline ink? If you have succeeded I think the same as the book made for B.B. would do for Bradban with 72 pages or if necessary with 48 pages only but with the paintless ink.

Re the animal figures, one set is under review with BB and it depends what they will decide in the next days. If they don't phone the order (the blue being very weak) we could then come in with our proposals, but naturally BB would at once know where the sketches came from and would have to be informed about our plans before we really can prove that Purnells can do offset work.

One can only assume that "Our mutual friends" refer to the three individuals mentioned at the beginning of this chapter.

Teleprinter messages, dated 20th.April 1937, between Wilfred Harvey in Paulton and Clifford Gibbs and Murray Thomson in London show that Wilfred Harvey was really looking at new techniques in great depth and from all angles; they also show that he was still upset with certain of his customers.

To Mr Gibbs
I had Budwig and son at the house to dinner last night in order to discuss things further. Our difficulty now is about the litho plate making and I told Budwig that I did not propose to put it in at the moment. He was rather surprised but took it well. Up to last night I had intended to ask Siviter Smith of Birmingham to make these plates but on second thoughts I think Jephcott may within a couple of months be able to do it.
(Jephcott was the director in charge of Bristol Photo Engraving, based at 35 Broad Quay, Bristol, a company in which Paulton Holdings already had an equity holding.)

The cost of the plant would be about £4000 but the difficulty would be to get really skilled people to take work here at Paulton. As you know, the artists, retouchers etc. are very temperamental people and I doubt if I could get them, now with Jephcott, they have all these people at present on process work, they also have cameras and various other work which could come in for both litho and process. I am therefore arranging for Budwig and son to spend the afternoon with Jephcott and see me again tomorrow –just a tic Budwig on the line.
Budwig brought down his enquiries from Birn; oh it is all a funny game when you hear the various stories. These publishers are a funny lot. However, he asked me to approach Birns and I told him that as he and Birns are friends, I would go to Morris and Monty and place my cards on the table and if, as I understand that they are both Jews and those on this side are anxious to help those from Germany, then now was the time for Birns to stand by Budwig. He is going to see Birns on Friday when I shall be in town and if he wants me to come along after he has broken the subject to Birns I shall be on call at London Office. I will come up on Thursday eleven Paddington, go to lunch with Hunter, come on to office in the afternoon make an

appointment with Grigg and Jackson, see JMT for dinner in the evening and discuss our points and then stay over until Friday for any other matters.

Wilfred Harvey asked Stephan Budwig to remain in Bath and to get quotations from lithographic suppliers in order to assess the total costs for setting up an offset plate making department.

This he did from the Cleveland Hotel in Bath, getting the letters typed then sent in for Wilfred Harvey to sign before mailing; the letters to German suppliers had English translations for Mr Harvey's benefit.

Dagobert Budwig returned to Germany to arrange his affairs and he wrote to Wilfred Harvey on the 30th.April 1937

Podbielski Allee 54
Berlin - Dahlem

Dear Sirs,

I herewith beg to inform you that I had to sever all my connections with the Berlin-Neuroder Kunstanstalten Aktiengeselschaft after having served them for over forty years. I wish to thank you for all your kindness and confidence you have shown me which I always appreciated.
With regard to my future plans I shall take the liberty of informing you in the near future. Pleased be assured that I shall always be gladly at your service. Any correspondence will reach me at the above address until further notice.

In the meantime I beg to remain, dears Sirs,

Yours faithfully
Dagobert Budwig

Wilfred Harvey replied on the 3rd.May1937

Dear Mr. Budwig,

        I have just returned from London hence the delay to your letter, I saw both Mr Morris and Mr Monty Birn on Friday and we had a very successful time. I told them I should leave the litho account entirely with you and they have promised to give you all their work
I saw your son this morning. He is now in the factory making out plans for the litho department and we hope to see you in the near future.

Yours sincerely

Wilfred Harvey

Plans were indeed being made, for cameras, plate graining, retouching sections, plate whirlers and an air conditioning plant for the litho pressroom. Stephan Budwig also recommended that two Roland, two colour presses be installed to join the two Harris presses. All of this was taking time and a problem was emerging in engaging the skilled staff required to run the department, despite advertisements in the News Chronicle and Daily Telegraph.

On the 20th.May 1937 a Mr. Leroy was engaged from the London area to run the Harris four colour offset press, his wage was £10 per week with Trade Union conditions, his starting date was Monday 7th. June 1937.
Litho plates were bought initially from suppliers such as Gilchrist Bros. Ltd. Leeds.

Stephan Budwig telephoned and wrote to many trade litho plate suppliers, seeking the best quality at the best price. His typical question was "Are you producing Mother Plates and Machine Plates for offset deep in a size 45.5"x 54". We enclose a book entitled "Lots of Fun" in four colour offset. Please give us your price for similar designs, 16pp.and 32pp. Please quote for machine plates extra.

LITHOGRAPHY AND THE BUDWIGS

Orders for offset work arrived from Deans and Birn Bros., but not without a few problems, as one would expect with a new enterprise: for example, Morris Birn sent a letter to Dagobert Budwig on17th. May 1937: -

Dear Mr. Budwig,

I am afraid you will not like this letter and although you are coming up to see me tomorrow, Thursday, I think it as well to write same, so as to avoid any possible misunderstanding in the future.
I have quite enough trouble in business without having any more heaped upon me.
Mr.Morris Birn does not forget. Mr. Morris Birn has a very good memory, but your memory seems entirely at fault.
We have done business together for so many years, that it seems farcical for me to have to tell you that I never accept stock before I have seen the finished editions, and moreover, you know full well that I want either proofs or pulls from the finished editions, so that I can put samples in the hands of my travellers and so start selling the editions. This has been our invariable rule with you and why you should want, all of a sudden, to change this I do not understand. Furthermore, you are entirely wrong when you say you are not supposed to stock the goods. That is what you are supposed to do. That is part and parcel of the arrangement with Purnells.
I certainly resent, when I send a message that I do not want any more at present, for you to send up a further 200 gross, which I have returned this day. You say in your letter, 'we shall continue to do so'. Well, if you do, they will again be returned. I want a chance to sell my goods before I have them here.
Now kindly understand this applies to all orders which you have taken and I repeat again it is part and parcel of the arrangement.

Yours faithfully

Birn Brothers Limited
Morris Birn

Whether this upset was due to a lack of communication on Wilfred Harvey's part or Mr.Budwig senior, exercising too much authority, we shall never know.

There is no doubt that the Budwig, father and son partnership, got Purnells off to a much quicker start in offset litho than could have been expected by other means.

Arising from the Budwig – Purnell association, Wilfred Harvey learned of the methods used by the German authorities to subsidise printed work done in Germany for sale in England, and decided to have a go at getting import tariffs imposed on such work.

On the 10th.September 1937 Dagobert Budwig wrote the following statement to assist Clifford Gibbs and Wilfred Harvey in approaching the Board of Trade with a view to stopping the importation of books printed in Germany: -

"In 1936 I took orders in England for approximately £25,000 for picture and painting books for delivery in 1936 and 1937.
In Germany the manufacturer gets a 45% bonus on the value of his invoices, after deducting the cost of cases and freight, for goods to be supplied to Great Britain. I understand that this bonus has been reduced to 40% in April 1937.

Suppose I get an order for £1,000 when I am paid for this by the British firm I hand to the bank the cheque. When I took the order I inform the Reichwisbschafts Ministeriums or the Goldiscountbank of the fact and claim my 45% bonus. Suppose marks to be 12.35 to the £1 then my £1,000 order is worth 12,350 marks net. The bank then pays me 5,557.50 marks or £450. In other words the German government subsidises me to this extent so that I can undercut English prices.

In addition the German manufacturers have special facilities for buying paper for these export orders which is roughly about 25% cheaper than the price of paper for the German home market.

For the sake of argument, imagine that the paper used on the £1,000 order amounts to £450, the German manufacturer would receive an extra bonus of over £100 in order to help him compete again more favourably with English manufacturers.

These orders, which are for children's story and painting books, are not liable for any duty whatsoever when they come into England.

Further, I want to point out that the wages of a camera operator and photo-litho retoucher in Germany are about £4.5.0 a week while in England the wages of the same workers varies from £5.10.0 to£7.0.0. per week. Machine minders on offset litho presses in Germany get between £4.10.0 and £5.10.0 a week, in England the rate is from £6.10.0 to £8.0.0 a week. Wages of other workmen are in the same proportion".

Mr. Budwig was very concerned in case his name came to light on this report as he had property still in Germany and Sperr Marks; the Nazi government had already blocked the personal bank accounts of the Budwigs.
Stephan Budwig had recommended that two Roland Ultra, offset presses be bought to join the two Harris offset presses, providing, that the printing plates would be interchangeable between all four presses.

It seemed a good idea to Wilfred Harvey that if the money the Budwigs had in Germany could be used to pay for the Rolands, and the Budwigs recompensed by Purnell, then the Budwigs problems would be considerably lessened. Wilfred Harvey received a letter from the Board of Trade dated 31st.July 1937, from J.R.C. Helmore, Private Secretary.

Dear Sirs,

Sir Edward Campbell has sent to the President of the Board of Trade your letter of 22nd.July 1937 and has asked me to consider the possibility of exempting from the provision of the Anglo-German Payments Agreement the proposed purchase from Germany *of certain printing machinery by Messrs. Purnell and Sons Ltd. Sir Edward has asked that a reply be sent direct to you.*

The President desires me to inform you that he has given careful consideration to the matter and he regrets that, for the reasons given below, the Board of Trade are unable to agree to the proposed exemption.

The Anglo-German Payments Agreement of the 1st.November 1934 provides that 55% of the calculated value of German exports to the United Kingdom must be earmarked to pay off exports of the United Kingdom to Germany. The transaction proposed by Messrs. Purnell and Sons ltd. would involve the export to this country from Germany of machinery, the value of which would necessarily be included in the total value of German exports, even though Germany would not receive full payment for it in Stirling. The Reichsbank would consequently have to provide exchange for the purchase of United Kingdom goods in respect of a transaction which had not furnished them with the normal amount of foreign exchange. It is known that, in general, permission for such transactions has been refused by the German authorities on these grounds.

Numerous requests have been made by both United Kingdom and German interests that particular transactions should be exempted from the provisions of the Government and the Board of Trade have made it clear to the German authorities from the outset that they could not agree to an equivalent deduction being allowed from the exchange earmarked for United Kingdom goods. There is a large number of firms and persons in the UK and Germany with sums lying blocked in Germany who would wish to transfer them to this country in the form of goods if permission were given for a deduction in respect of such transaction, and each deduction would mean a reduction in the amount of sterling available to pay for United Kingdom goods exported to Germany. You will appreciate therefore that any departure from the present practice would be likely to place in jeopardy the whole working of the Payments Agreement.

So, unfortunately the Budwig's money and property remained blocked in Germany, but the purchase of the two Roland Ultras proceeded.

LITHOGRAPHY AND THE BUDWIGS

The agent for Roland presses in the UK was Rudolph Braunmuller, based at 2 Sandland Street, Bedford Row, London WC1.

Stephan Budwig wrote to Braunmuller on the 4th.November 1937:-

Dear Sir,

When we entered new negotiations regarding Roland Ultra two colour presses, we investigated whether your Rolands would synchronise with the Harris Offset presses. You confirmed this and we are now surprised to find that this is now not so, especially with regard to the width which on the Harris is 41.5'', while you only mention 39''
This also applies to the maximum transfer size, which is over 2'' bigger than you want to deliver, viz-minimum 40.6'' while you state 38.5''. How can you explain this?
We must have the presses the same size as the Harris presses.

Yours faithfully

S. Budwig

The Budwigs worked hard in getting the litho department up and running as a self-sufficient unit, not depending on trade suppliers.
The cameras were all using glass negatives in the 1930's and Stephan Budwig devised his own method, known as the "One Shot" system or "OS" for short for retouching the glass negatives; it was kept very secret.

Briefly, the system involved shooting the coloured artwork through filters and direct screens onto the glass plates. The dark blue filter used for the yellow plate needed a ten-minute exposure. The glass negative was developed, washed, stopped, washed again then put in a Bichromatic bath which reversed the image by bleaching out the solids, after another washing the plate was exposed to light and a new image redeveloped. Prior to retouching, three preparing baths were used, coded P1, P2 and P3; P3 was a chrome alum hardener but the constituents of P1 and P2 were unknown to but three, the manager, the foreman and a certain Miss Grace Snelling.

It was claimed and proven that a 90% dot could be etched down to 2% without losing density and going grey.

It was not until 1944 that transparencies were used in the department on a job called "Film Review" from the USA.

A Krause Step and Repeat machine, model M100L was ordered on the 5th. July 1937 and a few problems were encountered with varying voltage surges in the factory, but were soon corrected.

The Budwigs settled down to life in England and as history records elsewhere, things were getting pretty horrific on the Continent, and when war broke out in September 1939, the Budwig family and Purnells had another problem to overcome. All Germans living in the UK were regarded as aliens and could be subjected to internment for the duration of the war. The Budwigs lived in Bath and as aliens their movements were severely restricted and monitored under the jurisdiction of the local Chief Constable, in this case The Chief Constable of Bath, but Paulton came under the jurisdiction of the Chief Constable of Taunton. The simple task of travelling to Paulton from Bath was becoming a nightmare because Stephan Budwig could be interred unless something could be arranged on their behalf.

The company wrote to Frank Medlicott M.P., a Somerset man, on the 21st. June 1940 who was the Company's solicitor in London, as follows: -

Dear Mr. Medlicott,

Re Mr Budwig, Mr Stephan Budwig and Mrs Budwig. I wrote to you on the 13th.June and understand from your office that you have been good enough to forward this to the appropriate channel. Since then the following position has arisen

LITHOGRAPHY AND THE BUDWIGS

a)   *Our works at Paulton are situated under the jurisdiction of the Chief Constable of Taunton who has given permission for the Budwigs to work at Paulton. Paulton, by the way, is a protected area.*

b)   *The Chief Constable at Bath has granted permission until the 27th. June for them to reside in their house in Bath but apparently he cannot give permanent permission for them to live at Bath because they are working in an area which comes under the Taunton Chief Constable.*

c)   *It would be normally a simple matter for them to leave their home in Bath and come to live nearer the works, but 1) Owing to the fact that the district round the works is a Reception Area, very many children from all parts of the country are billeted there and there is practically no possibility of three alien Germans getting accommodation. 2) Seeing the Chief Constable of Bath and the Local Tribunal know the Budwig family, they might just as well stay where they are and where they are known rather than move into a district where the Police and the residents have no personal knowledge of them at all. My request, therefore in simple language is this, that acting on behalf of Messrs. Purnell and Sons Ltd. and bearing in mind the reasons given to you in my letter of the 13th. would it be possible for you to use your influence with the Home Office and ask for permission to be given to the Chief Constable of Bath to allow the Budwigs to continue to live at their present address under his jurisdiction ?*

Yours faithfully

For Purnell and Sons Ltd.
PS Mr Budwig is over 70, Mrs. Budwig is 66 and Stephan Budwig is 37.

These efforts were to no avail at this stage and Wilfred Harvey sent a teleprinter message to the London Sales Office on the 4th.July 1940: -

'WH this end. Please give this to Mr. Biggs. Will he thank Mr. Medlicott for what he is doing on my behalf on account of Stephan Budwig. I believe Mr.Medlicott is in town today and I shall be glad if Mr. Medlicott will write to the Home Secretary asking him to grant Mr. Budwig permission to reside permanently at Wells or any other place as near as possible to Paulton and refrain from interning Stephan as I need his brains in this factory. I will also write to the Home Secretary and say that Mr. Medlicott, I believe, will support my application'.

This arrangement did in fact happen, the Budwigs moved to Wells, but only temporarily, they were soon back at Bath. The litho department grew on the firm foundations laid down by the Budwigs and Wilfred Harvey's determination to make Purnells a leading book producing house.

Stephan Budwig, on the right, on the occasion of his retirement in1962, receiving gifts from Bob Wilshire.

CHAPTER FIVE

THE WAR YEARS

Whilst the management of Purnells in the late 1930's was busy with establishing the new litho department, the rest of the established departments had not been neglected.

The composing department had grown in size in order to feed the ever-growing sheet fed letterpress department. The company had in use, by the outbreak of the Second World War, 16 Double Quad Crown Perfecting Presses, 6 Quad Crown Perfecting Presses and 4 Quad Demy Perfectors. In addition there were 4 Vertical Miehle presses and 3 Horizontal Meihle presses, for the production of covers and jackets, and 2 two-colour Quad Demy presses, and 2 two colour Quad Crown presses. Fred Harvey, Wilfred Harvey's brother and Works Manager, was responsible for all this and the bindery, ably assisted by his departmental managers. The presses had been repositioned into the recently erected buildings that had been built up to 1935 and the litho department was built to the north of these buildings and considerably lower, as the site slopes down towards the Cam brook.

During the latter part of 1937 the Cottrell, four colour, sheet fed, letterpress rotary machine was installed: Roderick Horne had persuaded Wilfred Harvey that perhaps two-revolution presses were a thing of the past, but he never rushed into things, everything had to be investigated thoroughly, such as the sales supply, the skills required, the maintenance, and buildings.

As with the offset litho presses, the supply of plates was the main concern for the Cotterell press and it required special skills to cast the curved plates and to pre-makeready them for the press. Roderick Horne had recommended to Wilfred Harvey that the firm of Nickeloid, or to give them their full title, The Nickeloid Electrotype Company Limited, based in Printer Street, London, E.C.4. would do the job very well.

Nickeloid acknowledged the first Cotterell job sent to them, "Children of all Nations" on 24th.January1938. The man at Purnells who was responsible for blocks, stereo plates, and now the curved Cotterell Plates, was Mr Dutton who had joined the Company in 1926 and served for 33 years. By early July, problems were encountered with the plates cracking on press, replacement plates also cracked. Nickeloid sent a letter to Purnell, on this subject, dated 15th. July1938:

Dear Sirs,

In reply to your letter of the 14th. instant concerning the curvature of the plates which we supplied to you in March last, we would advise you this matter has been referred to Mr. Corey our General Manager; he wishes me to say he will take an early opportunity of discussing this personally with Mr. Harvey, and he hopes you will allow the matter to lay in abeyance meantime.

At this juncture we would mention the point at issue is not a question of faulty plates, but is confined solely to the matter of curvature, and in this connection we followed the normal procedure.

Yours faithfully

Production

The problem of cracking plates and of having the correct curvature was sorted out and the press spent many successful years on bookwork.

The work going onto the Cotterell press left the 4 two-colour presses rather short of work, because on the 7th. October 1938 Wilfred Harvey wrote to Edward Hunter at the Sun Engraving Co. Ltd. in the Strand, London, this letter:-

Dear Hunter,

As I understand it, you are putting out the four page coloured insert of the Picture Post to various printers, may I venture to ask if you will give us a part of it? We have two Quad Crown and two Quad Demy 2-colour Miehle machines we could place at your disposal for the job, and we could arrange to work night and day.

Yours truly

Wilfred Harvey

David Greenhill, the Director and General Manager of the Sun Engraving Co. Ltd. replied on the 10th. October:-

Dear Mr. Harvey,

Thanks for your letter. Can you possibly come to Watford to see me tomorrow, Tuesday, about some urgent work in connection with Picture Post.

Yours truly
David Greenhill

Purnells printed 400,000 copies and bound 100,000 copies by the 28th. October 1938, but unfortunately had to give some credits for some errors in interpreting the pricing of the job.

1939 arrived, and the annual spring custom of many years standing, was to send a box of primroses to all Purnells customers. This year with its depressing European news, made these harbingers of spring even more welcome, as the following letters indicate:-

  Percy White of Sampson Low Marston & Co. Ltd.

Dear Mr. Purnell,

Once more the very much-appreciated harbingers of spring have come along. It is a very charming way of reminding us of the better weather after a long, cold winter.

With kindest regards to yourself and Miss Tapp.
 Christina Foyle, W.& G. Foyle Ltd.
Dear Sirs,
        Thank you very, very much for sending me that posy of primroses. It was such a surprise, and I do appreciate it.

Yours sincerely

 Christina Foyle

Dorothy Horsman, Victor Gollancz Ltd.

 Dear Mr.Harvey,
                Very many thanks for your card and the charming primroses. I much appreciate the graceful compliment.

Yours sincerely,

 Dorothy Horsman

 Beatrice Ridley, Methuen & Co. Ltd.

 Dear Sirs,
        I am desired by Mr. Philip Inman to thank you for your kind gift of primroses. They brought a welcome breath of Spring and the country into the office.

 Yours sincerely,

 Methuen

 David B. Murray, Sampson Low Marston & Co. Ltd.

Dear Sirs,
        I take pleasure in enclosing my company's cheque for £1,500 for the credit of their account. You will no doubt let me have a receipt in due course.

Let me take this opportunity of thanking you for the delightful box of primroses. Goodness knows how many years it is now since this touch was first introduced by your house.

Yours faithfully,

David B. Murray

A.H. Chapple, Marshall Morgan & Scott Ltd.

Dear Mr, Purnell,
I greatly appreciate the kindly thought which prompted the sending of a bunch of Spring flowers. I sincerely hope that the Spring will bring with it better times for all of us, and relief from the anxiety of recent months.
With all good wishes

Yours sincerely,

A H Chapple

There were many more letters of a similar nature, from grateful publishers.

The company's interest in gravure printing goes back, at least to March 1938, when Wilfred Harvey was having meetings with Mr. Soldan of Soldans Ltd., the agent for Miehle letterpress machines and Vomag gravure presses. Wilfred Harvey was exploring different methods of printing the "Magic Painting Books", but more of this in a later chapter.

The London Sales Office sent a teleprinter message to Paulton on the 29th. August 1939, " Mr Gibbs has just rung up to say that he met Howard Marshall by chance today and he has been broadcasting for the last few days to the Empire. He seems to think that things are a little brighter today internationally".

The following day Wilfred Harvey sent this teleprinter message to the London Sales Office, " W Harvey this end. This is a message for Mr Bradban. I have arranged to take a large house here in order that the staff of Deans can be evacuated and their work carried on from this end, there will be enough accommodation for 16 people. As to the Chase I have arranged with the authorities to accommodate six people, i.e. Mr.and Mrs. Bradban and Pamela and three others in addition the government have allocated to us three doctors who will be working in the district."

After Germany had invaded Poland, the country was partitioned between Germany and the Soviet Union, and Britain and France had declared war on Germany, on the 3rd September, Clifford Gibbs was still intent on business. He sent this teleprinter message to Wilfred Harvey at Paulton:-

Gibbs here. Did you know that all the Gollancz staff except the executive, i.e. VG, Miss Horsman, Norman Collins and the head of accounts and stocks departments have been told not to come up until the emergency is over.

I wonder too if Mr.WH and Mr. FH have considered the effect of the Russian-German pact on the Left Book Club? I believe there are a number of cancellations of membership from disillusioned and some life long left wing adherents. Also I believe that VG is holding up all further choices until he is able to know what to publish. Probably most of his left wing international books are already out of date politically. All he can do is to publish the home political books and even these obviously will need to be of a certain type.

Macmillan is holding up publication of the new Walpole book as they say that no one is buying at the moment.

Mr Roland Heath and Mr. Cusion are in charge of their air raid shelter and they will not be closing down in the event of hostilities. All the staff have been told to stay away for one day only and then to return. Mr Harold Macmillan, the Chairman was looking more cheerful this morning and the heads of departments are going to try and come up.

I think that is all the gossip there is".

The uncertainty and fear certainly caused the orders to fall away at the Paulton factory. Fred Harvey sent a message on the 6th. September 1939 to Murray Thompson (London salesman and later a director, retired 1966):-

"I spoke to Mr WH last night as to whether we could approach the Stationery Office in regard to printing and binding. At the present time we have very little work in hand, sufficient to last say not more than a fortnight or three weeks.

Mr WH asks if you could go along to the Stationery Office and see the Director of Printing and explain the matter, they know what machines we have and what we are capable of doing.

I would suggest that the Director of Printing or his assistant comes down here and looks over the works. It will give him some idea as to what plant we have. I understand that the National Register is being compiled and this will make an enormous lot of printing. We could cope with this work quite easily.

The point is, that the rest of the orders we have in hand, we may not be able to get paper, seeing that this is now under Control. We have a certain amount of paper for our own books, but where publishers are supplying it will be very difficult for them to get delivery.

There is an emergency agreement between the Master Printers and the Trade Unions, that we can put people on short time or even dispense with their services through this period and unless we can get hold of some work it will be necessary to do so".

The effects of the war began to cause problems for the Paulton factory and the Sales Office London, staff was being called up for National Service and bombs were falling around the London office and on the customers premises.

To add to the misery, the Air Ministry commandeered a new building that was under construction to assemble aero-engines and an engineering firm called Symonds Aerocessories was moved into another part of the site.

The former building caused a bit of a problem with the local council, this concerned the Public Footpath running through Pigeon Close. Wilfred Harvey had been taken to task before by the council, for erecting buildings that were not properly documented however, on this occasion he replied to Mr.H. H. Evans, clerk to the Paulton Parish Council, on the 20th.August 1940: -

> *Dear Sir,*
>
> *With reference to your letter of the 14th. inst., concerning the PUBLIC FOOTPATH in Pigeon's Close, we beg to advise you that the building in question is being erected on instruction from the Air Ministry.*
>
> *May I suggest that the new path be made between Mr.Turner's house and the end of the new factory? If this suggestion meets with your Council's approval I shall be pleased to meet any of your Councillors on the site to discuss the matter further.*
>
> *Yours faithfully,*
>
> *PURNELL & SONS LTD.*

One of the first staff members to get called up into the R.A.F. was Wilfred and Fred Harvey's brother Bert Harvey, who had worked in the Garland Department. Bert wrote to his brother Fred on the 23rd. August 1940, from R.A.F. Exeter: -

> *Dear Fred,*
>
> *You might have seen a letter, which our Squadron Parson wrote to W with regard to sending him some books.*
>
> *In this connection the Parson passed on this information to a Lord Dudley who is Commanding Officer of the R.A.F. training unit at Torquay. Unfortunately for me, Lord Dudley has asked me to try and get a few books for his men, which I promised to do.*
>
> *Could you help me in this respect? I don't suppose W would mind although I never expected the Parson to inform anyone else that you had been good enough to give this squadron books.*
>
> *We have plenty to get on with here. I hope to get home for 48 hrs. during next week.*
>
> *Dudley's address:-*

Squadron Leader,
Lord Dudley
R.A.F. Training Unit
Torquay
Your affectionate brother

Bert

In 1940 Clifford Gibbs also got called up in the R.A.F., to 101 Squadron at West-Raynham, leaving Murray Thompson alone in London to handle the Sales function of the Company and Juveniles together with Wilfred Harvey when he came up to Town.
The wartime exchange of letters between Clifford Gibbs and Wilfred Harvey gives a very good picture of the problems, not only being experienced at Purnells, but also throughout the country in the publishing and printing business, at this anxious time.

Wilfred Harvey to Pilot Officer Gibbs on the 13th.January 1941

I was glad to get your letter giving me news of your whereabouts and what you are doing.

I am not sure what the position is in regard to Morgan Marshall & Scott. When I go to town next week I hope to call on Mr. Chapple, meanwhile I can tell you that Coker was sufficiently insured. He was here on Thursday. Sampson Low and Sheed and Ward are in our London Office and Murray Thompson has gone over to Juveniles.

When I was in London, Percy White asked me if I was still interested in taking a controlling interest in Sampson Low and I said that, provided the terms were favourable, I should still be interested. He has promised to write to me and when I hear from him, I will give you the news in due course. I should very much like to get hold of Sampson Low as this would give us a jumping off ground for novel publishing.

The position of raw materials is now getting very serious. Most of my time is spent, not getting orders but in getting materials with which to execute the orders. However, we are still operating full time with the people we have.

I believe you know that Camelot Press was hit and that a couple of weeks ago I went to see Gollancz at his place near Reading. We have taken over the whole of the type from Camelot and are now busily engaged upon reprinting the titles which Gollancz badly needs. I had a very interesting and successful interview with Gollancz. For your information I enclose a copy of the Balance Sheet. You will see that the Annual General Meeting takes place on the 22nd. Inst.

Thompson is in Bristol until Wednesday. He has to make arrangements for his wife to be taken to the Chesterfield Nursing Home at Clifton, Bristol and for his mother to be evacuated to Bath. He proposes to come to the works on Wednesday.

Jackson and Kray are here today discussing the years programme with me.

I am glad to say Mrs.Harvey is very much better. I need hardly repeat that if your wife finds herself in an awkward position on account of the Blitz she need not hesitate to come to the Chase until you are able to find her other accommodation

I am enclosing your cheque herewith.

Kind regards

Yours sincerely,

W. Harvey

P.O.Gibbs to W.Harvey – 6th.February 1941.

Dear Harvey,

I had a great surprise this week. I walked into the Mess for lunch and who should be sitting there but your brother A.J. As you know I expect, he is in Bomb Disposal and had come to do certain jobs around here. Apparently he came a few weeks ago but I was away and missed him. We had a chat together and then he came down to my office and stayed on the premises for about an hour whilst some rather interesting things were done (which must not be put in letters) and then he had to go off with his lorry and party.

It seemed absurdly strange that we should meet again under such strange surroundings.

I have now been definitely posted here as Adjutant and shall be quite content to stay here in this particular job, because apart from the office work, it brings me into touch with all the men. I can make things a lot easier for the deserving ones – at the same time, I am the C.O.'s personal representative and everything and everyone who wants to contact him comes through me. In these days this makes the job a much more interesting one than an Adjutant's job in the Army in the last war.

I am glad to say that I am kept busy – office hours for me are 9 till 2.20 or later, 2 – 5p.m. and then generally 5.30 pm – 7.30pm.
In addition to this I am with the air crews – do P.T. with them before breakfast, play rugger and soccer with them, go for runs, etc. as the C.O. is tremendously keen on their being kept busy and fit.
I also see them off and stay up for their return, not because I have to do so but because I don't like the idea of sleeping, etc. whilst they are on the job.

I hope that you and Mrs. Harvey are well and that Eric, Geoff and Betty are getting on all right.

Please remember me to C.J. and Miss Tapp, Fred and the Birns.

I hear from Masters regularly, he is still on the anti-aircraft guns

All good wishes to you and Mrs. Harvey.
Yours ever,

J.C.Gibbs

Wilfred Harvey to P.O. Gibbs, 10th, February 1941

Dear Gibbs,

I was glad to get your letter of the 6th. you appear to have a strenuous but interesting job and I hope matters will go well with you.

The position here is that we have plenty of orders but very few men to execute the work. Week by week further people are leaving us and machines just remain idle.

By the way, the new building I put up has been commandeered by the Air Ministry and, in confidence; I think the Bristol Aeroplane Co. will be commencing an assembly plant very shortly.

As far as raw materials are concerned, things are getting more acute every week, but we must not grumble.

I have recently had an enquiry and I am going to London on Thursday to discuss the matter further with reference to printing Bank Notes for Thomas De La Rue. I am not very keen on getting the business only to the extent of being able to say that we have printed Bank Notes and know how to do the job.

I am more than anxious to keep the book business together and to safeguard our goodwill until the end of the war. One redeeming feature about Bank Note printing is that I can get regular supplies of paper, however, I have not definitely turned down the proposition and will let you know my decision in regard to this matter when I write again.

Jackson, Bradban and Birns are inundated with orders, in fact, they are taking far more orders than I can ever hope to execute but still it is better to see more orders than not enough. Prices are of course increasing, especially in the Juvenile market. What was 6d. before the war is now 9d. and the 1/- books are being sold at 2/-.

I trust your wife and kiddies are well.
With all good wishes to you

Yours sincerely

W. Harvey

THE WAR YEARS

<u>Wilfred Harvey to P.O. Gibbs 22nd. March 1941.</u>

Dear Gibbs,

Thank you for your letter of the 14th. I believe Rouse has already written to you in regard to your salary and Income Tax. So sorry to hear of the death of Dr. Stafford Clark's younger boy.

You have probably heard that Butler and Tanner have been taken over by the Ministry of Aircraft for some kind of air craft production, and people holding stores were told to take them away within 48 hours. We have arranged to take Marshall Morgan and Scott's hymn sheets which Butler and Tanner did for them. I believe Thompson has already arranged to take over certain stocks of Ward Locks and other publishers, and I believe he is seeing Hodders who might now wish to make use of us.

I am however, using my discretion, I am not prepared to undertake work for new customers. This is not the time to do so and would be unfair to our other customers who have been faithful to us in the past. However, I am, as already said, using discretion in this matter.

Mr. Smith of Jenkins, with Reece, was here the other day I showed them round the factory, Smith had no idea that we had such a large place and he was much impressed. I shall be going up to London on Wednesday next when I hope to have lunch with Smith, meanwhile we have more orders than we can tackle, but the raw material problem is getting extremely serious.

For your private information, the Bristol Aeroplane Works have taken over a portion of our Works but we are still able to function as printers and bookbinders and I hope to be able to carry on in order to preserve our goodwill until the end of the war.

We are all well at this end, and as to my family, Betty and Peter are at Wolverhampton, Eric at Weston- Super-Mare and Geoff is House Surgeon at Southmead Hospital in Bristol. I trust your family are well.

Kind regards
Yours sincerely

W. Harvey

P. O. Gibbs to Wilfred Harvey, 25th. April 1941.

Dear Harvey,

I wonder if you had heard that last week Bromley officially caught the full blast of that Blitz on London.

The Central Hall is non-existent and a number of other churches, such as the Parish Church, St. Marks the Congregational and part of the Methodist.

Our old road got it and Phyllis's previous home and her aunt's and sister's were among many others, which were burnt up completely.

I was thankful to have got Phyl and the children away, especially when I heard that in our own road, the house opposite was burnt out and that incendiaries were all around us. One of the golf pro's, with whom I used to play a great deal, has lost his wife and two babies.

Would you ask Rouse to make a note of my change of address. I was moved here three days after I had arranged for Phyllis to come away from Bromley. This week she moved again and is near me at the Vicarage in Aylsham.

We have had rather a sad time here but the way the others take it is marvellous. I can't see any end to it yet but in these days of modern warfare, things change so rapidly that I am hoping for a complete surprise one day.

If Fred has a spare moment, would you ask him if he could have a proof copy of two of Gollancz's books sent to me, one is by Bernard Newman about "Fifth Column Murder" and the other is by Dodd, the late American Ambassador in Berlin.

I hope that you are all well

Kindest regards to Mrs. Harvey
  Yours ever

  J.C. Gibbs

Flt. Lieut. J.C.Gibbs to Wilfred Harvey, 27th. September 1941
From RAF Horsham, St. Faith, Norwich.

My Dear Harvey,
                    I have just heard from Thompson about the fire.
I am so sorry that, in addition to all your many other problems,
you have now to carry this further complication. I do hope that the
damage is not too extensive or crippling. It seems too bad that just
at this time, when things are so difficult, you should have to scout
around for machines, which I imagine are almost unobtainable.
We have been having a busy time lately- but just at the moment we
are quieter. I have just managed to get Phyll and the children up
here in a small house near the aerodrome.
Everyone seems to think a renewed Blitz will start soon and we
feel it is safer here near the aerodrome (when I can sleep with
them frequently) rather than have them alone in Bromley.
  All good wishes to you all
  Yours ever

  J.C. Gibbs

Wilfred Harvey to Flt. Lieut. Gibbs 29th. 1941

Dear Gibbs,
                    The fire has certainly knocked me very hard. We have
lost the three colour process rooms, all the sewers,(sewing
machines) and all the folders. I am hunting through the country
trying to get hold of a few sewers and folders in order to keep the
main bindery going on a smaller scale. I can never hope to regain
our original position until after the war.
  Mr. Savery's machine room is still intact and so is the Litho room
and I hope to keep going until better times come along.
  I am glad to hear that you have been able to secure a house
nearby for your wife and family.
  With kind regards
  Yours sincerely
  W. Harvey

The Somerset Guardian reported the fire in September 1941 as follows:-

DISASTROUS FIRE: MUCH DAMAGE AT PURNELLS
Three departments were destroyed by a disastrous fire, which broke out at the Paulton printing works of Purnell and Sons Ltd. on Sunday night, before it could be got under control.
Valuable machinery was affected and several thousand tons of books ruined.   Damage done, runs into tens of thousands of pounds.

The departments burnt out are the Colour Room (where the fire started), the Folding Room and the Sewing Room.   Employees working as firewatchers discovered the fire at 9p.m. on Sunday. The new tender from Clutton RDC and also tenders from Midsomer Norton, Radstock, Bath, Keynsham, and Wells also attended the fire.   The water was drawn from Cam brook by hydrants; everyone in the neighbourhood gave a hand, but in half an hour the fire had gained a grip.   The flames coming through the roof of the Colour Room were visible for many miles around, the Folding and Sewing rooms then got involved.   The fire was finally brought under control in the early hours of Monday, in all, seven fire brigades were involved.
Much   valuable   machinery   by   American   and   German manufacturers was involved and is irreplaceable.
150 men and women have been found other work on the premises.
"We are definitely carrying on" said an official of the company, Mr, Wilfred Harvey, Mr. Fred Harvey and Mr. S.V. Wiltshire were also at the scene of the fire.

The Purnell engineering staff managed to recover and rebuild some of the machines damaged in the fire over the next few months and a little help was forthcoming from the printing trade, which sent along their surplus machines.

It took many months to get the fire loss information collected and into the hands of the publishers, as exact records did not exist. The

lost material included standing type, printed sheets of paper, plain paper, and books in various stages of production.
The tidying up and clearing the site also took a long time and used up labour.

This photograph, taken by a member of the staff, with a simple camera, shows the devastation caused by the February 1941 fire at Purnell's factory at Paulton.

The war was having a unsettling affect on Purnell's publishing customers, some were getting bombed, especially those in London, those with book clubs were finding membership reducing in numbers and in one instance, the owner was called back to his country, the USA, on urgent government business.

Murray Thompson wrote to Wilfred Harvey on the 14th. June 1940.

Dear Harvey,

SHEED AND WARD

Following our teleprinter messages yesterday, I think it is interesting to say to you that, whilst it is true Sheed continues to owe us over £12,000, we have now got from him a Debenture of

£6,000 on the English business, a kind of lien on his shares in the New York business and the sole interest in his personal life insurance.

In addition to this we have today had from him his positive assurance that the interests of Sheed and Ward in England are to him, as he put it, " the apple of his eye".

Both Pratley and I this morning were very impressed with the man's honest intentions and we do believe that the result of his journey to America would be that Sheed and Ward would be able to publish where some of the English publishers would have to "dry up" and that he will ensure a really firm cash payment to us from America.
I think we have reason to be pleased at the result of our call this morning. Pratley and I have worked together on the suggestions and what one did not think of sometimes the other one did.

> *Yours sincerely*
> *JMT*

William Foyle (W & G Foyle Ltd.) to Wilfred Harvey
23rd. September 1940.

My Dear Harvey,
> *I am writing to ask whether you would be good enough to help me over a temporary difficulty.*

As you probably know the post is upside down and we are getting it four and five days late and unfortunately, instead of receiving the whole lot, we then only get one day's post which means quitea financial set back to me by way of Book Club 2/6's.
We have just met £2,000 of your Bills last week and wondered whether you would be able to discount another one for me, for £1,000, letting me have a cheque for the amount. At this time, I would appreciate it very much indeed if you could see your way clear to help.

Thanking you for your kind past favours.

> *Yours sincerely,*

> *W. Foyle*

<u>J. C. Gibbs to Wilfred Harvey, 30th. September 1940.</u>

Dear Harvey,

Sampson Lows had a bomb very near to them last night and the whole of their place has been affected by blast. The building itself is intact but there are no windows and the doors have been blown etc.

Will you please arrange not to send anything up to Lows until you have further instructions. Mr. White will be asking us, I think, to deliver everything direct but until he has had the chance to look round he wont be able to give us any definite instructions.

We understand there is a time bomb on the railway just outside Paddington but we have no confirmation.

> *Yours sincerely,*

> *J.C.G.*

P.S. We had another bomb near St. Paul's last night it burnt out a famous old pub "The Black Swan".

<u>Murray Thompson to Wilfred Harvey, 25th. November 1940.</u>

Dear Harvey,

> *(1) Would you like to buy Gilbert Foyle's interest in the Foyle Companies? As a matter of fact if you would let me arrange an interview with Samuel, to be followed with lunch with Gilbert Foyle and Samuel,*

while, without any doubt, the proposition would not interest you, it would give you the chance, I think, of getting a real inside view of the Foyle construction and finances.

(2) There is a Foyle Bill falling due on the 7th. December for £1,500. William Foyle has asked Samuel to ask me to ask you if you would postpone this a fortnight. What instructions please?

Yours sincerely,

J.M.T.

On October the 10th.1940, three bombs had fallen very close to Foyles, one fell on the opposite side of the road, another hit the building in which Mr. Samuel had his office, the third landed in the middle of the road between Foyles old and new buildings. The building was not destroyed but the windows and doors suffered.

Wilfred Harvey declined the offer to buy Gilbert Foyle's interest in the business.

At the end of 1941 the number of companies, fully owned by Purnells, that supplied printing orders to the Paulton factory, was six. They were, JUVENILE PRODUCTIONS, BRITISH GREETING CARDS, SOVEREIGN BOOKS LTD., PAPER NOVELTIES LTD., HARRY GREEN (Publishers Ltd.), and T.T. MACDONALD & CO LTD.

The Company also had made investments in other companies that supplied services to the Paulton factory.

The Cotterell, sheet fed, letterpress rotary press, had it's curved plates supplied by The Nickeloid Electrotype Company Limited, which had it's Head Office at New Street Square, London EC4. This supplier wrote to Purnells on the 6th.October 1941.

Dear Sirs.

On the 23rd. July 1941, you were informed that the Nickeloid Electrotype Company Limited had been placed in voluntary liquidation and that the liquidator was in negotiations with important interests with a view to establishing a new company.

Unfortunately the enclosed communication from the liquidator has been made necessary by difficulties which, despite persistent and intensive efforts, obstruct the reconstruction of NICKELOID in the immediate future, and which seem to be insurmountable.

Whilst certain important units of the original electrotyping plant have been recovered, it is not possible in these days to procure the additional units vital to a complete foundry conformable to NICKELOID ideas.

And so it is with great regret that I have to inform you that from Wednesday, 15th.October next is the last day upon which the company can accept orders. I assure you, however, that although trading will cease at that date, all orders then in hand will be properly completed.

Please accept my warmest appreciation of the support the company has enjoyed from you.

Very truly yours

J. A. Corey

The directors of the Nickeloid company at this time were, Nigel De M. Bond, O.B.E. , Major John S. Crosthwaite Eyre, O. E. Crosthwaite Eyre, J.A. Corey(General Manager), G. Orford Smith, and Adam Maitland.

Eventually the control of Nickeloid came under the Purnell management and part of it moved to the comparative safety of the Paulton site, so that curved letterpress plates for the Cotterell press were still available.

CRASHING DOWN—masonry of a bombed building near St. Paul's brought down during demolition.

A newspaper picture sent to Fred Harvey by Murray Thompson in June 1941 with the following postcard message.

Dear Mr. Fred,

I enclose a picture of London Office, which, quite seriously, I suggest is interesting enough for you to have framed and put up in your palatial establishment at Paulton.

I might mention the heroic figures in the foreground are Mrs. Copland and myself anxiously waiting to get to work.

The Heroism of Purnells London staff is beyond all praise. Fortunately we have had to stand so many blows from the Works that the mere fall of a bit of masonry just bounces off our hardened skins.

Tough we are my boy!

Yours sincerely

J. M. T.

Fred Harvey, who was managing the Paulton factory, and Murray Thompson in London, who had been transferred to Juveniles, also had their fair share of problems too, as their correspondence reveals. Thank goodness they both had a good sense of humour.

<u>From Murray Thompson to Fred Harvey, 7th. January 1941</u>

PITY POOR LONDON OFFICE

No teleprinter.
Only one phone and that intermittent.
Letters, four to five days late.
Suburban train service already bad, practically impossible through snow, (I came up by car, 15 miles in second gear, including an incredible traffic jam on a steep, slippery hill).
No heating in our office.
Two people with chesty colds spreading germs.
No gas.
No lavatories.
No hot lunches within two miles.
But there will always be a Purnells!

Yours sincerely,

J.M.T.

The deputy overseer of the letterpress department, Albert Fear, completed his 50 years service with the company in November 1942.
He had joined the company in 1892, when the total staff of the company was only six and he was 14 years old. There was a special presentation made to him by Clifford Purnell, the Company Chairman, of £500, £10 for every year that he had worked for the company.

This early 1940's, aerial photograph of the Purnell factory is believed to have been taken by the Bristol Airplane Company before they moved into the building on the extreme right.

CHAPTER SIX

BRISTOL PHOTO ENGRAVING

The Bristol Photo Engraving Company Ltd. was one of the first companies to be invested in by Paulton Holdings in 1936.

The company was based at 35 Broad Street, Bristol, in a building complex that it leased from the St. John the Baptist Church on a 75 year lease, due to expire on the 25th. September 1943. The rent was £212 per annum, due in four equal payments.

The business was to supply process blocks to the printing industry.

The company was incorporated on the 26th. March 1920, with a capital of £7,000. The shareholders of the company were:-

a) William Coker Iliffe
    Caundon House,
    Coventry.
    Certificate No. 7 100 x £1 shares
    Certificate No. 4   1 x £1 share

b) Edward Mauger Iliffe
    Allesby Hall, Nr. Coventry
    Certificate No. 8   100 x £1 shares
    Certificate No. 5   1 x £1 share

c) Joshua Spencer Bold
    14 Chester Street, Coventry.
    Certificate No.1   1 x £1 share

c) Archibold D. Poulton
   Penhurst, Barras Lane, Coventry.
   Certificate No. 2   1 x £1 share

Edward Mauger Iliffe became the first Baron Iliffe in 1933 (Proprietor of the Birmingham Post and Mail Ltd. and Coventry Newspapers Ltd.) as well as many other business connections throughout the country, including part ownership of the Daily Telegraph.

Further shares were issued on the 7th. November 1923 to Greyfriars Ltd., 15-16 Buckingham Street, Strand, London. Certificate No. 3 & 6 to 6505, inclusive, fully paid.

On the 10th. March 1924, 295 shares of £1 each, certificate Nos. 6706 to 7000 inclusive were issued to Greyfriars Ltd.

The signatories to these last two issues to Greyfriars were, William Coker Iliffe and Edward Mauger Iliffe, as directors of Greyfriars.

Greyfriars Ltd. sold the business in 1927 to Herbert Mathew Dodwell of 54 Oakfield Road, Clifton, Bristol.

The purchase agreement is interesting in that the business was to be sold for £17,000, the purchaser wished to borrow £17,000 from the Bristol Photo Engraving Co. Ltd. in order to pay for the purchase of the shares and the vendors had agreed to repay a £5,000 loan that they had borrowed from B.P.E., they therefore had agreed to lend £12,000 to B.P.E. (to be secured by Debentures charged on the assets of the company). If the purchaser's remunerations from salary, commission or dividends from the £7,000 of shares exceed £1,000 in any year then this surplus is to be used to purchase from the vendors one or more of the said Debentures. B.P.E. to issue a certified copy of the Trading Account and Balance Sheet, half yearly, until all the said Debentures have been redeemed

By 1931 the directors of the company appear as Julian Hoare and E. C. Jephcott and remained so until 1935, the directors in 1936 were W. Harvey and E. C. Jephcott.

On the 22nd.March 1938, Mr Pocock, the accountant for Iliffe's wrote to E. C. Jephcott, the manager of Bristol Photo Engraving, from 16 Buckingham Street, Strand, London WC2: -

"I enclose deeds and documents as shown on the attached schedule, in regard to the original lease of your offices and works at 35 Broad Street, Bristol, you will notice that Lord Iliffe and Mr Coker Iliffe are guarantors to the lease. Now that they have no longer any interest in the business, I suggest that arrangements should be made to release them from the guarantees, say by substituting Purnell & Sons Ltd. This matter should really have been dealt with when you and Mr. Harvey purchased the business. Perhaps you will have a word with Mr. Harvey on this subject."

The sales figure of B.P.E. in the year 1931 was £5,085

1932	£4,772
1933	£5,753
1934	£N/A
1935	£8,022
1936	£9,998

The profits of the business went to Paulton Holdings each year in the form of dividends paid on the equity holding, not every year produced a profit, for example in 1940, a loss of £947.18.4 was made.

On the 25th.September 1940, the German Air Force increased its bombing attacks against Britain's aircraft industry; this of course, included Bristol or Filton in particular, which got severely damaged. Several more attacks in the following months did tremendous damage to Bristol City itself.

During the war, as the lease was due to expire on the Bristol premises, and coupled with the bombing of Bristol, arrangements were made to relocate BPE at Paulton. When the gravure plant was established at

Paulton, BPE became the gravure pre press department, although always regarded as a separate company, which in fact it was.

Bristol Photo Engraving was in existence well before it was incorporated in 1920 and reproduced here is a sample of their half tone letterpress block making, taken from the 1911/12 edition of the *Penrose's Pictorial Annual.*

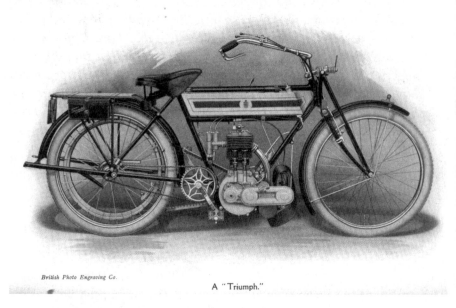

British Photo Engraving Co.

A "Triumph."

1911: Bristol Photo Engraving's example of a vignetted, half tone, letterpress block.

It is interesting to note that, of the two illustrations displayed in the 1911/12 *Penrose's Pictorial Annual,* the company name is presented as a Limited concern on only one and this may indicate that the company initially, became a limited company in that year of 1911.

The Bristol Photo-Engraving Co., Ltd.   *Photograph by C. H. Horton.*

The Chapel of the Gaunts, Bristol.

A photograph which required an exposure of six days.

This Chapel is situated in the Mayor's Chapel, Bristol. and is of great historic interest. The dimly lit Chapel, with its beautiful detail carvings and monument to departed worthies, is a sight not easily forgotten.

Another incredible piece of work of the Bristol Photo Engraving Co. Ltd. A letterpress halftone block of a photograph that took six days to expose! This illustration also appeared in the 1911/12 edition of *Penrose's Pictorial Annual.*

The BPE Company's letter heading in March 1940.

The BPE Company's letter heading in May 1940

PURNELL AND SONS
LIMITED

BOOK AND MAGAZINE PRINTERS
COLOUR PRINTERS
AND
BOOKBINDERS AND STATIONERS

WORKS

PAULTON
NR. BRISTOL

TELEPHONE
MIDSOMER NORTON
96 AND 97 (TWO LINES)

ST. PAUL'S CHAMBERS   19 LUDGATE HILL
LONDON E.C.4

Directors :

C. J. PURNELL (Chairman)
W. HARVEY (Managing Director)
J. C. GIBBS
F. A. PRATLEY, F.C.A.

TELEPHONE : CITY 2382/3.   TELEGRAMS : " EXELPRINT CENT, LONDON "

JMT/JS   16th May, 1938.

The parent company letter heading in use at roughly the same period as those above

98

CHAPTER SEVEN

THE POST WAR YEARS

The years from 1945 to 1960 saw another large growth in the company from an investment in machines, acquisition of like companies, and a profit generation aspect.

The staff was returning from their wartime national service from 1945 to 1947, including managers and directors and confidence was returning to the publishing world. However, material supplies were still terribly short and this factor alone was responsible for the acquisition of certain Purnell Group companies.

During the war years the Company ran a "Comforts Fund" for those away on active service, who were connected to the letterpress departments, and this was largely organised by Mr. F.C.Collyer the Father of the Chapel. The bindery had a similar scheme that was organised by Mr Albert Carter of High Littleton. At one time, the binding department was sending 150 comforts out to members in the forces. The funds were wound up by a New Year's Eve dance 1945/46.

The Bristol Airplane Company took their Engine Fitting Department back to Patchway in June 1947. A farewell party was held in the Works Canteen and about 120 attended.

Bristol Photo Engraving had moved from Bristol into the old buildings of Park Corner at Paulton, when their Bristol lease had expired in1943. Nickeloid Ltd. also was incorporated into the Purnell Group of companies in 1944, and was sited at Paulton, just above the old fire centre.

In 1945, Purnells acquired the controlling interest in the gravure printing company of L.T.A.Robinson Ltd., based at Cranmer Road, London SW9, in a 64,450 sq. ft. factory on a 1.31-acre site. The property was leasehold with a ground rent of £11,200 per annum; the lease was for 30 years.

Wilfred Harvey's daughter, Betty Jean Rogers Harvey, had met and married a management trainee from Mardon Son and Hall, called Peter Lavington, just before the war. After his demobilisation from the RAF, Peter Lavington joined L.T.A. Robinson as a manager and eventually succeeded the firm's founder as Managing Director.

L.T.A. Robinson Ltd. was one of the country's leading mail–order catalogue, gravure printers and Peter Lavington's technical knowledge on this matter was extremely good, he was one of the first to install Autotron controls on gravure presses and the use of electronic scanning on a commercial basis. He joined Purnells in 1961-62 to plan and install the new Purnell gravure project, later managing the concern.

L.T.A. Robinson had three gravure presses, two with 45" wide paper webs and the third with a 30" wide maximum web. These presses could get through 20 tons of paper in 24 hours. The company made it's own ink, but had no bindery, so the Paulton factory did the wire stitching ,trimming and despatching for them.

During the war years, paper rationing was a major problem for all in the printing trade. It was based on a percentage of paper consumed by the user in the year preceding the war, this applied to publishers as well as printers. Fortunately, Purnells had some publishing companies, but a 50% cut in paper hurt badly and limited production.

S. V. Wilshire the Company Secretary, was greatly involved in the procurement of materials during and after the war. This involved waste paper saving and repulping, even organising the collection and delivery of straw after the local harvests to the mills for straw board. In some instances, heavy weight paper was sent to the mill to be repulped and remade into lighter weight paper, which gave more sheets to the ton. S.V. Wilshire was also responsible for getting the manufacture of ink done on site at Paulton.

In 1946, Purnells still short of paper, bought the R. Somerville & Co Ltd. paper mill at Creech St. Michael, Somerset. This mill was producing about 35 tons of paper a week and was in need of modernising.

Better methods and replacing worn and old parts increased the mill's output. The stock preparation beaters were removed and a hydrapulper and refiners put in, a supercalendering unit, a cutter and high speed reeler, and a paper conditioning plant for litho papers was also installed. The steam engine that was driving the paper making machine was replaced with a variable speed electric motor. By 1954 the output of paper had risen to between 70 to 80 tons per week.

The lithographic printing company of Henry Hildesley Ltd., who specialised in point-of-sale advertising material, was also purchased in London. No initial changes were made but gradually Purnell changed their programmes to suite the work supplied.

The Chairman of Purnell & Sons Ltd., Clifford J. Purnell, attained his 80th. year in 1945 and retired from the business.

On the 26th. April 1947 the 13th. Annual General Meeting of the Company was held at the Chartered Insurance Institute, 20 Aldermanbury, London EC2.

The Directors of the Company were:
W. Harvey   (Chairman and Managing Director).
J. M. Thompson
J.C.Gibbs
S. V. Wilshire
W. F. Harvey
E. R. H. Harvey, M.C., M.A., B.C.L.
Bertram Clarke (Company Secretary)

The new directors were S.V. Wilshire who had been the Company Secretary and had been with Wilfred Harvey since before Purnell had become a limited company. Eric Rogers Hammond Harvey was Wilfred Harvey's youngest stepson, a practising barrister, who had just left the army with a Military Cross awarded during the Arnhem campaign in the advance on the Elst crossroads in 1944. Wilfred Harvey persuaded his stepson not to resume his career in law, but to join the Purnell publishing subsidiary company of Macdonald in London. Bertram Clarke was a chartered accountant, a Manchester man who moved to the West Country in 1927, and worked for the same firm of accountants as did Wilfred Harvey in Bristol. He joined Purnells in 1945.

At this point in the company's history it is interesting to look at the profits generated, particularly the 1940's, the war years, on a yearly basis;

The profit for 1935, the year of incorporation, was £34,324.

1940	£29,000
1941	£54,416
1942	£220,000
1943	£380,000
1944	£428,585
1945	£815,133
1946	£988,005
1947	(£1,229,590) 1 yr.= £983,676
1948	£801,954
1949	£571,950

Note that the figures above, for 1947, relate to a financial year of 15 months as this was the first time that a Consolidated Balance Sheet, accounting for the subsidiary companies had been produced.

The current assets of the company in 1947 amounted to £2,429,037 against current liabilities of £1,823,454.

THE POST WAR YEARS

One of the reasons why the profits during the war years were so successful was the Company's ability to get paper. Paper rationing was in force for the industry and initially it was based on a percentage on how much each company had used prior to the outbreak of the war. This also applied to publishing companies, and Purnells had Juveniles, Macdonalds and Paper Novelties.

Investment in new machines for the pressrooms and the bindery certainly benefited from the profits generated

In 1947 two new Harris offset presses were bought from Smyth-Horne Ltd. One was a 34"x 45" single colour press, the other a 42"x 45" four colour press.   The bindery received a McDonald film-laminating machine that put a protective, plastic film, onto book covers and jackets. A Sheridan perfect-binding machine with the then novel, rotary gathering machine attached. This latter piece of equipment had a series of warning lights on each gathering station, which indicated mismatches and missed sections, it was promptly christened "Blackpool Lights" by the bindery staff, a name that stuck well into the 1970's.   Two Sheridan, gather-wirestitch-trim machines were bought to handle the increase in this type of work, particularly that from L.T.A.Robinson Ltd. The letterpress department received two Cotterell four colour, sheet fed, rotary presses.

The fall in profits for the years 1948 and 1949 was explained in the annual report and accounts for these years as being due to material and labour cost increases not being passed on to the customers to preserve their goodwill. In January 1949, 300 staff was made redundant. This large number reduced the staff level to approximately 1,200, the reason given in the local newspapers for the redundancies, was a dramatic fall off in orders. The Company made the position clearer with a press statement, the following week, by emphasising that the dismissals only mainly affected temporary and part time workers, some of which had been engaged in 1948 to man extra shifts during the fuel economy measures. The fact is, the Company continued, is that we are now employing 20% more staff than in 1945

The publishing house of Sampson Low and Marston had belonged to two men, one died and the remaining partner was Percy White. Percy White had asked Wilfred Harvey to buy his shares, at a time when he was suffering from ill health and the shares were in fact bought, bringing the company under Purnell's management control. David White, the son of Percy white was now running Sampson Low and one day Clifford Gibbs introduced the children's author, Enid Blyton to him.

The outcome of this meeting was that the "NODDY" series of books came to Purnells for printing and binding for many years alongside the many other well known titles produced by Enid Blyton. In 1949 the Paulton factory was honoured with a visit by Enid Blyton and the following photographs record that visit, department-by-department and machine-by-machine.

Bert Chivers correcting and making up a page of type matter for a Blyton Title, prior to stereotyping.
The page of type matter and line block is held together by page cord, clearly seen around the page in the photograph.

Purnells had been making their own flat stereo plates for many years but casting curved plates for the Cottrell press called for a little more expertise and that was provided by the Nickeloid Company.

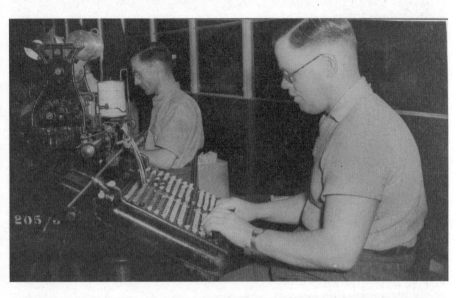

George Beale at a Monotype keyboard, working on an Enid Blyton manuscript.

Enid Blyton has a go at "cleaning up" a curved Cottrell letterpress plate in the Nickeloid Department prior to sending it to the pressroom.

Cliff Comer, the Cottrell minder, is telling Enid Blyton how to print 16 pages in four colours at 4,000 sheets an hour.

Children waiting to get their signed Blyton books from the author.

We don't know whose protective hand is appearing behind Miss Blyton's back!

Fred Harvey, the Works Director, explains the workings of a Smyth, model 12, book sewing machine to Miss Blyton. Fred was the brother of Wilfred Harvey and the father of Bill, Maurice and Charles Harvey.

Peter Pickering, in the background, seeing that Joe Wiltshire is not overstating the complications of a Smyth 24 casing-in machine to Enid Blyton.

Lots of happy children getting their copies of the "Fourth Holiday Book" signed by Enid Blyton at the end of a successful and happy visit to Purnells at Paulton.

The Enid Blyton books came to Purnells from Sampson Low and Dean Son & Co. and continued for many years, well into the 1980's.

Mr. Charles Harvey, one of the sons of Fred Harvey, held some important positions in the publishing businesses of Purnells. It will be remembered that Wilfred Harvey was offered the opportunity to purchase Percy White's holding in Sampson Low during the war, and he accepted this offer, thus gaining control of an important publishing house.

Charles Harvey joined Sampson Low in the early 1950's as Editorial Editor and was instrumental in building up the business by making a success of "Noddy Library". He also built up the children's encyclopaedias, such as the pictorial range. He became General Manager of Purnell Bancroft in 1967, succeeding Charles Fisher and took control of Sampson Low, Bancroft and Adprint Publicity

Products, all of which became known as Purnell Books. Charles Harvey became Publishing Director of Purnell Books in March 1967. Another of the achievements of Charles Harvey was the development and expansion of the Walt Disney titles on the Purnell List. Purnells had been associated with Walt Disney since the 1930's.

Television, as it became more readily available to the general public, created some very popular children's characters that made excellent subjects for books and Purnells were not slow in suggesting that these Annual Books would be a good thing for all concerned ie, the children, the publishers and Purnells.

Thames Television used Charles Harvey at one stage to act as an adjudicator in a children's storybook writing competition, there were two age categories, under 10years old and between 11 and 16 years old. Two of the titles from the competition were actually published.

Annual sports books also became popular, again, no doubt to the ever increasing sales of televisions.

The bindery at Paulton at this time started to gain it's reputation as experts in casing-in thin children's books. By thin, we are talking about casing-in 16pp. and 24pp. books, using printed-paper laminated covers, over 3mm. boards and board spine hollows for the cases.

The casing-in machines were Smyth, model 24's that had been finely adjusted by the Purnell Engineering department. This department also made the special rotary board cutters for making the board hollows for the cases.

Eventually, Purnells installed two Smyth Automation Lines that enabled Flexi lined and trimmed books to be, cased-in, jointed and pressed, in one pass through the binding line.

Purnells acquired the Somerville Paper Mill at Creech St. Michael, near Taunton in 1946, Wilfred Harvey had been troubled by material shortages throughout the war years that had prevented him from achieving his targets and decided to take some positive action to ease the situation.

The Paper Mill at Creech St. Michael in 1947

The boilers for steam generation, not only to dry the paper but also to drive the paper-making machine

Incoming materials being hoisted into the mill, the chimney is belching black smoke. A railway branch line served the mill, which was convenient in the days when the boilers were coal fired.

The Somerville staff integrated well with the Paulton people and participated in Paulton's Sports Days with a mean Tug-o-War team.

112

The incoming wood pulp is beaten, and mixed with water, to produce porridge like substance called "stuff" at the wet end of the paper-making machine.

A thin layer of "stuff" is transported away on an endless wire belt to be pressed dry.

The dry end, after a lot of squeezing between rollers and heated by steam rolls, the paper is becoming recognisable.

The paper comes off the papermaking machine and is reeled into master rolls.

From here the paper can be split into smaller rolls or cut into sheets as required by the printer.

The edges of the roll, called the deckle, is trimmed off and repulped in the wet end, so not too much is wasted.

Purnell in their Envelope and Printing departments used Somerville paper right up to the late 1980's.

CHAPTER EIGHT

THE 1950'S

This decade brought about increased capital investment in plant and other allied companies.

The group profits for this decade, before taxation, were: -

1950	£561,001
1951	£441,938
1952	£358,861
1953	£551,097
1954	£603,962
1955	£627,357
1956	£643,938
1957	£712,385
1958	£711,781
1959	£735,589

There were more books produced in this decade than ever before or after, with a peak of 26,584,998 cased books bound in 1957, plus a further 5,294,989 limp bound books.

Paper prices went up by nearly 50% during 1951, a fact recorded in the company's Annual Report and Account for that year. The general increase in costs that arose in this decade were not passed on to the customers in their entirety, but absorbed as far as possible and offset by increased efficiency.

1952 and 1953 saw the introduction of a new packaging department situated in the Paulton factory. The new company was called Runprint, unfortunately, delays in delivering some of the new equipment, delayed full production until 1955. Runprint manufactured envelopes, waxed wrappings, film and foil laminates, printed by multi-colour gravure or by the Aniline process. A story once circulated that the company was successful in obtaining an order for toffee wrapping papers, the production went fine apparently, until it was discovered that the paper would not stay twisted around the toffees but kept unravelling. Attempts to get the correct paper were foiled as it was discovered that other competing manufacturers had cornered the market and Purnells were not allowed in.

House building and purchasing, for employees, reached a peak in the mid 1950's. Further investment in allied businesses continued also, particularly in the paper mills such as British Board & Paper Mills Ltd. from 1955 to 1957.

Sadly Mr. W. F. Harvey (Fred) died in 1958, he had been with the company since 1928 as a manager and as a director since 1945. It was Fred who carried the great responsibility of getting the manufacturing units through all the problems arising from the war of 1939-45, such as labour shortages, paper rationing, factory space commandeering and new regulations coming out at regular intervals on almost every aspect of factory life.

The major items of new machinery bought during the 1950's were: -

1950	2 X Smyth No.2 Case Making Machines.
	Smyth Jacketing Machine.
	2 X Darkroom Cameras.
	1 X Harris Single Colour EL Offset Press.
	1 X Harris Single Colour LSB Press.
1951	1 X Timson all size Rotary Letterpress Machine.
	1 X Hadego Phototypesetting Machine.
	1 X Sheridan End feed Case Making Machine.
1952	Timson Rotary Letterpress Machine.

Smyth No. 24 Casing-in Machine.

1953   1 X Roland size 7, four colour offset press.

Gula Varnishing Machine.

Smyth Model 45 Pressing and Jointing Machine.

2 X Opladen Spectral 4 Col. Web-Offset Presses.

(These were for printing cloth books)

1954   Roland size 7, four colour Offset Press.

1955   Dexter Case Making Machine.

1956   2 X Smyth No. 24 Casing-in Machines.

2 X Smyth No. 2 Case making Machines

1957   Darling Glue and Glitter Machine.

MAN Model ov15, 5 colour-offset press (41x56 inches)

1958   Vertical Projection Unit.

1959   1 X 6unit Photogravure Press. (Ex. L.T.A.Robinson.)

2 X Brehmer folding machines

2 X L & M two colour letterpress machines

The supply of materials, especially paper, to keep the expanding business running at full capacity, was an ever- present problem. To alleviate this, Wilfred Harvey continued to invest in British paper mills. In 1955 substantial investments had been made in the British Coated Board & Paper Company, but full control was not obtained until December 1961. This company had it's head office in London and owned a coating factory in South Wales plus associated companies, such as the Barrow Paper Mills, Rishton Paper Mills, Dowdings Limited of Derby and D & S Ockleston Limited of Parlington, Manchester.

Barrow Paper Mills operated two paper making machines with deckles of 120 inches, and two machines with deckles of 82 inches, producing wood free printings, machine finished litho papers and imitation art and writing papers.

Rishton operated two machines with 95 inches wide deckles, producing banks, fine printings, cartridges, writings and duplicator paper.

Dowdings operated one machine of 108 inches deckle and produced machine glazed, pine and imitation Kraft.

Ockleston operated one machine of 90 inches deckle producing the strongest Krafts (Golden-Browns), Light Manilas and Rope Browns.

When Purnell took control of the group they sold the coating plant in South Wales, but took much interest in the other companies, making the Barrow Paper Mills the major paper mill of the group. Wilfred Harvey's youngest son, Dr. Geoffrey Harvey became the Managing Director of Barrow Paper Mills.

Raphael Tuck & Sons Ltd., a publisher of postcards, greeting cards and books, was another company whose shares had been acquired on the open market, but Purnell did not get a controlling interest until 1961. This company had been a customer of Purnell for many years and Wilfred Harvey had persuaded Jackson, their production manager, to join him as publishing manager, when he launched Juveniles back in 1936.

Back in the Paulton factory, in 1951, the production of books was continuing at a rapid pace, as the following photographs show.

Offset plate making in 1951
From l.to r. Mr. Dobson, Fred Crook and Horace Wessell.

Pop Geoghan and Frank Sullivan in 1954

Roland Ultra four colour press, with Alan Watts in 1954

A Harris four colour press with H. Wessell and P. Batt in 1951

Daisy Chivers on a Camco SC8 folding machine in 1951

Folding Department 1951: Mr. Thatcher and Gert Beacham in the background.

E. Shearn, Gwen Fooks, P. Kingman and J. Barter, on a book-gathering machine.
The job on the machine has been printed two-on and will be split into two.

Dexter case-making machine 1951

Case-making department 1951: Smyth case making machines.

The sewing room in 1950, mainly Smyth machines.

The installation of the first Brehmer automatic sewing machines with Hepp feeders.

L. to R. Des Smith, Ted Sampson and V. Evans on a BMC Flexiback lining machine in 1951. There were several of these machines placed between the sewing department and the three knife trimming machines.

F. Curtis, R. Shearn and Peter Pickering on a Smyth 24 casing-in machine.

A. Honeybun and E. Raikes examining and stacking books from the Smyth model 45 pressing and jointing machine in 1951.

The packing department in 1951: Binders parcels being hand made and labelled. These parcels were often hand loaded onto the lorries, as mechanical handling had not yet taken off, particularly with the London publisher's warehouses.

The works canteen in 1951, there was another room for the managers and yet another for the directors and visiting customers.

There were people in the 1950's and 1960's, who predicted the demise of the book, due to the popularity of television, which was becoming more readily available to the population at large. The strange thing was, as far as children's books were concerned, that the reverse happened.

The children's favourite T.V. characters created an increase in annuals and holiday books such as "Muffin the Mule", "Sooty" (the Teddy Bear with personality), "Pinky and Perky", "Andy Pandy", "Windy Miller" and many more.

There were books to suit most pockets, from the small Tell Me A Story series, with a size of 4,75 inches square with a page content of 32 pages in full colour, to the more expensive Finding Out series with a size of 12.25 inches by 9.75 inches, making 80 pages. The former costing 1/- and the latter 13/6 in the 1960's.

This aerial photograph was taken in 1952 for inclusion in a brochure in the annual report and accounts. The swimming pool is shown in the top right hand side of the picture, with the paths leading down to it.

Also seen in this photograph are the magnificent elm trees soon to be devastated by Dutch Elm disease, and although not pertinent to the history of Purnells, a good view is given of some of Paulton's notable buildings, such as the old boot factory, now a residential area, the church, the Manor Farmhouse and the Red Lion public house.

The binding of mail order catalogues at Paulton became an important part of the business, mainly for Littlewoods and Great Universal Stores. The catalogue sections were printed and folded, usually on the press, by various British printers and several continental ones, mainly from Italy and Germany, and delivered to Paulton for storage, prior to the binding operations.

The catalogue publishing houses had their own binding styles, Littlewoods preferred their catalogues to be gathered and side wire stabbed, before the cover was attached. Great Universal stores, with

127

Kay's catalogue, preferred to have the printed sections thread sewn before attaching the cover.

Catalogue binding was seasonal; the two production periods ran for six weeks in June and again in December. One can imagine what a huge warehousing exercise this was and the production planning had to be precise so as not to upset book publishing customers or mail order customers with missed delivery dates.

Bill Harvey was the director in charge of mail order catalogue production; Mick Hewish ran the warehousing side and the recording of incoming sections, and heaven help any printer that was late on deliveries! Ken Bateson and subsequent other production managers spent many hours trying to dissuade the works manager not to fit in bookwork jobs that might be the last straw etc. The bindery manager, Bert Alderton, had to engage temporary staff, on all three shifts, and work lots of overtime to complete his schedules. The bookwork was mainly done on the night shift, operators from all shifts were multi-skilled and many men found themselves running sewing machines during catalogue periods.

The personnel department had the job of arranging the temporary staff to do the portering and lifting of the catalogues around the bindery. Where possible the student sons and daughters of the work force were used during the school and college summer and winter holidays. John Raine, who worked in personnel for many years, told an amusing story of a twin student who was engaged on catalogue work who bemused the factory staff by apparently forgetting everything he had been told the previous day and ignoring his newly made friends, until it was discovered that he was swapping shifts with his twin brother whenever he felt like a day off.

CHAPTER NINE

THE 1960'S

So much expansion took place at Paulton and within the Purnell Group in the 1960's that it is difficult to comprehend how it all could have been planned, actioned and controlled, largely by one man, Wilfred Harvey.

During one of my talks with Wilfred Harvey at the Chase, in the 1980's, he told me how he came to take control of the Waterlow & Sons Ltd. Group of companies. In 1960 he was invited to take tea with Sir Isaac Wolfson who had interests in Waterlows. Wilfred Harvey had known Sir Isaac Wolfson through his involvement in the printing and binding of the mail order catalogues for Great Universal Stores. It transpired that Sir Isaac was having some difficulty over the nature of the business and the Bankers involved, and asked Wilfred Harvey to bid for Waterlow & Sons Ltd. After careful, detailed research into the Waterlow companies, Wilfred Harvey acquired a controlling interest in them for Purnells, but not without a struggle.

In March 1960, Purnell & Sons Ltd. made a bid for Waterlow & Sons Ltd. of £2,150,000 through the bankers Henry Ansbacher & Co. The bid was for £540.000, 6.5% Non Cumulative Preferred Ordinary Shares, and £69,000 Deferred Ordinary Shares. Suggested terms gave a value of 22/- for the Preferred Ordinary Shares against the previous quotation of 18/6. The Deferred Ordinary 45/- against 41/- quoted. The Purnell Ordinary Shares fell by 6d. to 16/6.

On the 19th. April 1960, H. Ansbacher, acting for Purnells, declared their offer unconditional, for the capital of Waterlow. The offer was extended to the 26th April 1960.

Mr. Phillip Waterlow, the Chairman of Waterlow & Sons Ltd., attempted to reorganise the company, by varying the voting rights in order to escape the unsolicited advances of Purnells.

Mr. Ansbacher again wrote to Mr. Phillip Waterlow to say "we are to inform you officially on their behalf, that on the 19th. April when their offer to Waterlow shareholders was declared unconditional, that they were disposed of more than sufficient shares to defeat the proposed resolution, varying the rights, including voting rights of shareholders. Acceptances of the Purnell offer received up to today were above sufficient to defeat the resolution and a large number of further acceptances have been and continue to be received. In these circumstances, you will no doubt, want to reconsider your announcement that your Board intends to proceed with their proposed "reorganisation".

On the 21st. April 1960, a special Waterlow Board Meeting decided to ignore the Purnell letter of 19th. April 1960.

By the 13th. May 1960 the exchange of correspondence made it clear that the struggle still went on. A letter from H. Ansbacher to Phillip Waterlow, points out that valid proxies are held for 25% of the Preference Shares and more than 25% of the Preferred Ordinary Shares and a substantial number of the Deferred Shares. These will be used to vote against the Waterlow resolutions at the Waterlow meeting on 18th. May 1960, to consider the capital scheme. In addition we are aware of a number of proxies on the company's proxy forms, which will be similarly utilised. Evidence to support these statements can be made available, providing that Waterlow agrees to co-opt on to the Board a suitable number of Purnell representatives.

Mr. Waterlow's reply said, "As it appears that a substantial majority of the equity holders have not accepted the Purnell offer made, his Board feel unable to accept his invitation".

At the all-important meeting held on the 18th. May 1960, Purnells defeated the Waterlow resolution for capital reorganisation by 628,627 votes against 613,554; a very small margin.

Discussions took place between Purnells and the Waterlow Directors and an important section of those Deferred Ordinary Shareholders who had not accepted Purnells offer, and agreement reached on the reconstruction of the Waterlow Board.

The new Board of Waterlow & Sons Ltd. will consist of:

Mr. Wilfred Harvey	Chairman	(Purnell)
Sir Harold Gillet	Vice Chairman	(Waterlow)
Mr. E. W. Smith		(W)
Mr. Rupert Waterlow		(W)
Mr. Geoffrey Cameron		(W)
Mr. R. D. B. Todd		(W)
Mr. J. C. Gibbs		(P)
Mr.S. V. Wilshire		(P)
Mr. E. R. H. Harvey		(P)
Mr. L. A. Hart	(Ansbacher)	

The managing Director to be nominated by the Chairman and Vice Chairman and appointed by the Board.

The following relinquish office:

Mr. Phillip Waterlow	Chairman and MD of Waterlow
Mr. H. H. Todd	
Mr.J.W. Patterson	
Mr. J. F. Nye	

In addition to payments in satisfaction of their service agreements, which are terminable on 12 months notice, it is proposed, subject to the shareholder's agreements in general meeting, to pay compensation for loss of office as follows:

Mr. P. Waterlow	£8,000
Mr. H. H. Todd	£3,300
Mr. J. Patterson	£2,300

The following companies and properties now came under the management of the Purnell Group:

Waterlow House,
Worship Street,
London EC2   109,300 sq. ft. in .80 acres   Freehold

Cheque Factory
Vandy Street,
London EC 2   40,000 sq. ft. in .22 acres   Freehold

11/16 Snowden Street,
Alabaston Building,
London EC2   4,350 sq, ft. in .32 acres   Offices

28 Scruton Street,
London EC 2   5,200 sq. ft. in, 13 acres   Freehold Garage

Blomfield House,
85/86 London Wall,
London EC 2   33,000 sq. ft. in .21 acres   Leasehold Offices

Twyford Abbey Road,
Park Royal,
London NW 10   110,800 sq. ft. in 3.08 acres   Leasehold

George Street,
Dunstable,

Bedfordshire	394,000 sq. ft in 14.21 acres	Freehold Factory.
Scanden Works, Mary Street, Hyde, Cheshire.	35,400 sq. ft. in .96 acres	Freehold Factory
Peel Park Place, East Kilbride, Lanarkshire	100,250 sq. ft. in 6.58 acres	Leasehold
Sports Ground, Dunstable	9.9 acres	Freehold
Sports Ground, Chingford Road, Wathamstow E 17	6.76 acres	Freehold
109 The Headrow, Leeds	1,500 sq. ft. Lock up shop	Leasehold
31 North John Street, Liverpool	375 sq. ft. 4th.century building	Leasehold

At the Purnell Annual General Meeting held on the 29th. September 1961 the Chairman, Wilfred Harvey, reported in his statement:

"You will remember that during 1960 we were successful in securing control of Waterlow & Sons Ltd. At that time we had voting control only through the Preference and Preferred Ordinary Shares in that company. I am pleased to be able to report that we now hold a much larger proportion of the Deferred Ordinary Shares. As has been reported, Waterlow & Sons made a loss for the year to 31st. December last, and we are not, therefore, able to enjoy any profit from this company in the account you have before you. I am happy to report however, that since we became interested in this company and placed behind it the experience of our organisation, its trading conditions have improved, and it is now operating on a profitable basis. We hope to include a substantial profit in respect of your company's interests in Waterlow & Sons Ltd. in the Consolidated Account for 1961".

The Chairman continued:
"I have to report that before the Chancellor of the Exchequer introduced his interim budget we had committed ourselves to a large capital programme within this Group for our expanding Packaging, Photogravure and Rotary Litho Divisions.

Considerable improvements have in recent times taken place in printing machinery construction, and you have always supported your Directors in their view that this Company should be in the forefront with such developments. To finance this programme we propose, at an appropriate time, to raise further capital, and when this is done, whether in the form of a Rights Issue or Loan Stock with Conversion Rights, such capital will be offered in the first instance to our shareholders.

During the year we decided to launch a weekly magazine for children, printed in colour by lithography, and the first number of "KNOWLEDGE" was launched in January 1961 with the support of a most distinguished advisory editorial board. That there was a need for this unique venture in educational publishing, presented in a manner to stimulate the interests of boys and girls, has been proved by its success. The magazine, which is designed to grow into an encyclopaedia, has been welcomed widely by parents and teachers and has added considerably to our publishing goodwill.

You will wish, I am sure, to know the position of our trading during the coming year, and I am glad to be able to report that the trading of the Group for the current year is in excess of the corresponding period of 1960. We have, however, now to meet immediately very much greater direct labour costs in consequence of national agreements with the unions associated with the printing industry, which were negotiated before the government's recent economic measures. It remains to be seen how far the additional costs can be met by more efficient methods, which is the constant aim of the Company's management.

The rate of increase of direct wages in recent years, and the extent of the installation of capital equipment taking place in European countries, underline most emphatically the importance of ensuring that the Company's plant and methods of production are completely up-to-date.

I wish to pay tribute to my colleagues on the Board, all of whom are full time executives, and to express my thanks once again to the staff and all our employees for their services and co-operation. It has been a period in which they have been called upon to assist with success from their wide experience gained in our own organisation in widening fields of printing and publishing".

It is worth noting that Wilfred Harvey firmly believed that Company Directors should be working full time for their specific business and not have other part–time directorships that might distract their attention, and although offered other directorships himself in unrelated businesses, he turned them all down.

The part-work "Knowledge", referred to in the Company's Annual Report and Account, was printed sheet fed on the Roland presses at Paulton.

Back at the Paulton factory, the new developments referred to by the Chairman, were the introduction of web-offset printing to produce the new educational, part works each week and the construction of a very modern gravure factory, to be at the leading edge of technology in all areas covering solvent recovery, ink manufacture, cylinder preparation, press operation, paper storage and handling, pre-print colour inserts and print finishing.

An Allied Type Founders (ATF), Five Unit web-offset press was installed next to the sheet fed litho room. The Company had experimented with web offset back in 1953 when it installed two

OPLADEN SPECTRAL four colour textile presses to print rag books for Dean & Sons Ltd. Mr. Budwig and Mr. Draper had tried long and hard to make them work successfully but they had to admit to defeat, apparently the special ink required was a closely guarded secret in the textile business. Eventually a second ATF, five unit, web offset press was purchased to cope with the increase in part work production and other longer run publications better suited to the web offset process.

At the Annual General Meeting of the company on the 29th. September 1961, Wilfred Harvey outlined his large capital expenditure programme for a new packaging factory at Norton Hill for Runprint, Photogravure printing and Web offset printing.

Although Purnells had moved into the photo gravure field with the acquisition of L.T.A.Robinson in London, the benefits of comparatively cheap land and building costs with an on-site bindery already in existence to finish the operation at Paulton, made the whole, new gravure scheme, very attractive.

In 1959 a six-unit gravure press was transferred from L.T.A.Robinson to Paulton, primarily to train future machine minders in the gravure process. It printed Magic Painting books and Colouring books. I am told that the Purnell staff, always ready to identify a new entity, christened this press "The River Boat", it was disposed of in 1961.

The first Cerutti Roto Gravure Press was installed in the new Gravure building in 1962, it cost £238,103-10.

By the end of the 1960's decade, the Corporation was a huge enterprise; employing close on 20,000 staff and 20% of this was the Purnell Group, which excluded the Waterlow Group and the Publishing Companies.

The following chart shows exactly how the various companies were allocated to a group, led by a group Director, it also shows how many staff were employed, subdivided into the following categories:

Craftsmen
Apprentices
Male Assistants aged over 21 years
Male Assistants aged under 21 years
Female Assistants over 18 years
Female Assistants under 18 years

The count date was September 30th. 1969

Company	Crafts-men	Appren-tices	Other Male Wkrs. Over 21	Under 21	Female Wkrs. Over 18	–18	Total	Previous Quarter
PURNELL GROUP								
Purnell & Sons	413	41	680	77	566	50	1827	1777
B.P.E.	107	21	17	1	1	-	147	141
Western Ink	23	-	7	3	2	-	35	34
Clarke & Sherwell	74	19	69	3	34	-	199	199
Petty & Sons	164	19	220	4	169	31	607	574
L.T.A.Robinson	132	7	101	-	9	-	249	249
Somerville & Co.	64	4	6	-	18	1	93	92
Nickeloid Ltd.	454	13	150	10	20	3	650	656
Dovetail Press	10	-	-	-	-	-	10	10
Strand Lithographic	Sold						-	29
Group Totals	1441	124	1250	98	819	85	3817	3761
SUN GROUP								
Sun Printers	1120	75	1483	11	300	13	3004	3091
Hazells Offset	160	12	160	4	121	2	459	436
Group Totals	1282	87	1643	15	421	15	4363	3527

WATERLOW GROUP

Waterlow & Sons

Worship Street	350	22	267	42	178	25	884	944
Dunstable	292	35	342	6	235	26	936	954
Park Royal	226	-	477	-	2	-	705	711
East Kilbride	40	-	159	1	2	-	202	211
BPC Business Forms Leeds	57	6	95	1	69	20	248	251
BPC Business Forms Dunst.	39	3	162	16	88	13	321	316
Rocappi	1	-	2	-	2	2	5	5
Group Totals	1005	66	1504	66	576	84	3301	3392

PUBLISHING GROUP

BPC Publishing	-	-	258	10	347	18	633	618
Haymarket	-	-	187	19	142	4	352	352
Group Totals			445	29	489	22	985	970

PACKAGING & PAPER

Beric Press	27	8	54	4	10	-	113	108
Chromoworks	57	16	99	3	64	5	244	241
Fell & Briant	32	10	49	5	115	-	212	215
Henry Hildesley	54	7	70	11	70	2	214	196
Taylowe Ltd.	123	26	338	11	151	30	679	659
Cross Paperware	17	6	160	20	256	22	481	444
" " Cleator	53	-	43	13	56	20	185	191
Harold Wesley	57	1	81	11	161	29	340	346
Barrow Paper Mills	19	3	223	31	140	22	438	469
Jas. Broadly Ltd.	44	13	78	5	78	10	228	223
B. Taylor & Co.	24	8	27	3	46	3	111	104
Rishton Paper Mills	11	-	105	4	36	1	157	159
Group Totals	528	98	1327	121	1183	144	3401	3355

BOOK PRODUCTION GROUP

H.W.V. Ayles.	445	56	588	38	373	46	1546	1552
H.W.V.Cymer	31	5	37	14	162	37	286	269
W.& G. Baird	39	7	25	1	27	2	101	102
Dorstel Press	128	21	106	2	232	15	504	510
Tonbridge Printers	72	13	32	-	33	6	156	157
Group Totals	715	102	788	55	827	106	2593	2815

LETTERPRESS GROUP

F.A.Clements	58	14	12	2	23	3	112	117
Gale & Polden	135	21	178	5	92	8	439	464
Keliher H. & K.	106	17	81	9	23	-	236	242
Sidney Press	99	10	28	-	38	3	178	176
BPC L/Press	-	-	23	-	10	2	35	31
Group Totals	398	62	322	16	186	16	1000	1030

NEWSPAPER PUBLISHING

Bird Bros.	19	6	20	-	11	-	56	59
Clare Son & Co.	33	5	15	1	10	-	64	62
Kentish Express	23	5	24	3	26	-	81	84
Group Totals	75	16	59	4	47	-	201	205

PRINT HOUSE

	-	-	49	-	32	3	84	73

CORPORATION TOTALS

	5444	555	7387	404	4580	475	18845	19270

The following photographs show the construction of the gravure factory, it's equipment and some of the staff involved in running it. Bristol Photo Engraving, was run as an independent profit centre, to make the gravure cylinders, store them, and reuse them. Gravure ink was also to be made and piped into the presses, on the Paulton site. solvent recovery was to be of the latest and most efficient equipment available.

The boiler house, ink factory and solvent recovery plant nearing completion during the winter of 1960/61.

1961: The newly finished building, a very impressive photograph. The tree on the extreme right of the picture was the last Elm tree to be felled on the site in 1974 when it became a danger to the building.

Above Cerutti presses 1, 2 and 3 and press 4 below in a very modern setting.

Peter Lavington joined the Board of Purnells in 1962. He was very knowledgeable on the technical side of gravure printing and cylinder preparation; he was regarded by his peers in the industry as a pioneer in the development of scanners in this country. It has been said that he was the ideal man to have been put in charge of Purnell Gravure.

In Bath on the 18th.March 1970 Peter Lavington gave a lecture to the South Western Branch of the Institute of Printing, entitled "Gravure in the 1970's"

He was made Joint Managing Director of Purnell in1970 but sadly died at the early age of 60 on December 20th.1974, after a six months illness, leaving a widow and a daughter. Peter Lavington had married Wilfred Harvey's daughter Betty just before the out break of the war.

In the early1960's Purnells entered a joint venture with the Observer newspaper to produce a weekly magazine to accompany the Sunday Observer; it was to be printed by gravure. Purnell had three Cerutti presses up and running and were awaiting the delivery of press number 4, in July 1969, which would enable the Observer Magazine to have 96 pages, 72 of which would be in colour. Unfortunately the lorry transporting units 12 and 13 had a crash on the Italian side of Mount Blanc, totally destroying the units and three crates of rubber coated rollers. The installation was not unduly delayed as the press started up with eight units whilst waiting for the other five to be repaired and delivered.

The 35 tonnes load of units 12 and 13 of press No. 4 spread over the road somewhere in the Alps in 1969.

With all the increased printing capacity installed, the composing department began to feel the pressure. In August 1964 the Company purchased a Linofilm system; the keyboard and film unit cost £31,288-13-11. To this was added an Elektron Mixer in March 1965, plus extra matrices, another keyboard and in May 1965, a Lino Sec with mixing parts, which cost another £21,260-19-7

The Daily Express pre-print start up. From left to right Vic Sherwood, Brian Shales, David Dereham, Charles Carpenter, Eric Bugden and Les Eardly.

The Observer Magazine celebrates printing over a million copies for the Svetlana Stalin issue, on the 24th. September 1967, with an on-site visit.
From left to right: Eric Harvey Managing Director, Charlie Carpenter Gravure Manager, Mr. Tristan Jones General Manager Observer Magazine, Victor Bishop Managing Director of B.P.C.

In 1962, in the most northerly reaches of the Purnell Group, Wilfred Harvey was acting as host to some very important guests, at the new East Kilbride factory.

Her Royal Highness Queen Elizabeth II and the Duke of Edinburgh were to visit the new factory that printed the Radio Times, on the 2nd. July 1962.

Captain J.C.Stewart presented Wilfred Harvey to the Royal party, Lord Lieutenant of the County and Wilfred Harvey accompanied the Royal couple throughout the various departments, demonstrating the equipment and answering questions.

Within the Waterlow group of companies were two factories that printed the Radio Times and other publications for the British

Broadcasting Corporation. The Park Royal Factory, situated in Twyford Abbey Road, Park Royal, London, NW 10. and the East Kilbride Factory, which printed the Scottish editions, situated at Peel Park Place, College Milton, East Kilbride, Scotland.

The Radio Times, in the mid 1960's, ran to four and a half million copies weekly. The page content varied from 52 pages to 72 pages and there were nine different regional editions.

July 2nd. 1962 The Royal visit to the East Kilbride printing works that produced The Radio Times. The Queen and Prince Phillip leaving with Wilfred Harvey after an interesting visit.

At the Annual General Meeting held on the 28th September 1962, Bertram Clarke and William J. Harvey were appointed to the Board, and at the Extraordinary General Meeting that followed, Peter Lavington and A. C. Grant were also made Purnell directors.

In 1963 Purnells acquired the whole of the Issued Capital of the two printing companies Gale and Polden Ltd. and Fell and Briant Ltd.

These companies were letterpress houses, Gale and Polden was based in Aldershot, and were involved with printing local newspapers, periodicals, and magazines. They were pioneers and experts in printing with sheet fed, rotary, letterpress machines, using wrap round Dycril plates in 1964 and Nyloprint plates from 1969. In 1973 they won the Printing World award for the best sheet fed rotary letterpress work, with their entry The London Illustrated News.

Fell and Briant specialised in labels, again by letterpress, although in the coming years they introduced litho and gravure presses.

An event took place at 4.20 pm.on the 5th. December 1963, in another printing concern that created major interest throughout the whole of the British printing industry.

Geoffrey Crowther, who had only been appointed Chairman of the Hazell Sun Group, ten days since, went into Lesley White's office, the Managing Director of the Hazell Sun Group, to announce that a bid for Hazell Sun had been received from "The News of the World". The Carr family owned the News of the World.

The Hazell Sun Group Board regarded this bid as a hostile one, for several reasons, not least that the balance of photogravure printing capacity in Great Britain would be upset. Hazell Sun were believed to have about 50% of the capacity, International Publishing Corporation (Odhams) 35% and the "News of the World" subsidiary company Bemrose, the remaining 15%. Purnells at this time were very small in gravure. Purnells and Hazell Sun had already held talks in the past about the possibility of working together, as both printing groups were developing on parallel lines.

The N. o W. bid was for nearly £11,000,000, which equated to a share value of 21/-

Wilfred Harvey and his colleagues with Henry Ansbacher as adviser met the Hazell Sun Directors whose adviser was S. G. Warburg, and the outcome was a joint statement that a marriage between the two groups was felt mutually necessary, if only to prevent two-thirds of the country's photogravure capacity falling under the control of one management, so a counter offer would be solicited.

The statement contained some salient points:

The two companies whose combined market capitalization approached £27.000.000 are planning to amalgamate under the title of the "British Printing Corporation". Negotiations have been proceeding between the two boards for some time but have been accelerated by the approach to Hazell Sun Ltd. by the News of the World Organisation. The Hazell Sun share price had risen to 23/4.5 by the Stock Exchange close on 4th. January 1964. At this stage there were no terms revealed of the proposed merger. A few days later, the Purnell Group bid nearly £13,000,000 for Hazell Sun. The terms of the bid were, two Purnell shares plus 30/- in cash for every three shares of Hazell Sun. This offer valued the shares at 24/6 each, comfortably topping the earlier bid of 21/- per share by the News of the World Organisation.

The News of the World Organisation quickly retaliated by stepping up it's bid by offering two Ordinary Shares plus one Non-Voting Share in the News of the World Organisation and 156/- in cash for every nine Hazell Sun Shares, this valued them at 27/- per share.

The main surprise in the renewed News of the World bid is that the formal offer documents from Purnell show that over 50% of the Hazell Sun shareholders have indicated that they are prepared to accept the Purnell offer. These include Mr. Max Rayne's London Merchant Securities, which has a 30% stake in Hazell Sun (these shares were bought from the Daily Mirror Group and Thomson Organisation in early 1963 for £1,400,000 and were currently worth £3,000,000.)

The News of the World Organisation Ltd. published a notice in the press in January 1964 as follows:

An Announcement

The
News of the World Organisation Ltd.
advise
Hazell Sun
Shareholders

Not to accept the Purnell offer of approximately 24/6 per share for Hazell Sun Ordinary Sares before they have considered the News of the World offer of 27/- per share, which will be in their hands next Thursday morning. The News of the World Directors give this advice to avoid the possibility of any Hazell Sun shareholder accepting the Purnell offer and subsequently being refused permission to withdraw his acceptance and thereby being deprived of the benefit of the higher price offered by the News of the World.

In a circular sent to Hazell Sun shareholders, explaining why the Directors recommended the Purnell offer, Sir Geoffrey Crowther said: "In coming to their decision we think that shareholders will wish to take into account some factors other than their own financial benefit. One of these factors is the desirability in the public interest of there continuing to be a large periodical business independent of the newspaper publishers. It will not be a good thing for the freedom of the press in this country if anyone wishing to start a new magazine, to compete with the existing ones, is virtually compelled to go to one of his prospective competitors to get his printing done".

The News of the World Organisation Ltd. published a statement in the press in late January 1964, "We have reluctantly decided to withdraw from negotiations for Hazell Sun Ltd., as it appears impossible for the News of the World Organisation now to acquire a majority holding.

The News of the World Organisation's proposal to offer a price of 27/- per Ordinary Share of Hazell Sun far from being "frivolous" as Sir Geoffrey Crowther, Chairman of Hazell Sun Ltd., is reported to have described it, was based on a detailed knowledge of the photogravure printing industry and an expert appreciation of what Hazell Sun would have been worth as part of a general integration with Eric Bemrose Limited. As such integration and the progress which would have resulted therefrom would not be possible without control of Hazell Sun.

The News of the World Organisation are not interested in acquiring a minority holding.

The Directors of the News of the World Organisation regret that a large number of shareholders of Hazell Sun have been deprived of the opportunity of accepting an offer of 27/- a share.
"

It is interesting to note, that in 1968, a member of the Carr family who owned 25% of the shares in The News of the World, wished to sell his holding and had promised to sell them to Robert Maxwell. After a lively shareholders meeting in 1969 Mr. Rupert Murdoch gained control of the Sunday newspaper.

As if Wilfred Harvey did not have enough problems to cope with, he had the misfortune to lose his eldest stepson Geoffrey Harvey in 1964. Geoffrey Harvey, a doctor of medicine, was the Managing Director of Barrow Paper Mills at the time of his death.

The shareholders had approved the merger of the two Groups on February 6th. 1964; the Directors of the newly created British Printing Corporation Ltd. were not appointed until a meeting held on March 12th. 1964, no reasons were given for the months delay.

At this meeting questions were asked about the Directors remunerations and no specific information was received until March 22nd.1965, over a year later, when a schedule was produced.

The first Directors of the British Printing Corporation, elected in February 1964 were:

DIRECTORS

W. Harvey *(Chairman and Managing Director)*
Sir Geoffrey Crowther *(Vice Chairman)*
J.C.Gibbs
E.R.H. Harvey M.C. M.A. B.C.L.
Max Rayne
Elliott Viney
L.G. White
S.V.Wilshire

JOINT SECRETARIES

Bertram Clarke F.C.A.
E.A.Corp F.C.A.

The Registered Office of the Corporation was The Works, Paulton, near Bristol.

The first Annual General Meeting was held at the Connaught Rooms, Great Queen Street, London, W.C.2 on the 28th. September 1964. The notice of the meeting nominated it the thirtieth annual general meeting which it was for the Purnell Company.

The Chairman's statement explained again how the Purnell Company had changed its name as had been circulated to both groups' shareholders in January 1964.

Purnell and Sons Ltd. changed its name to The British Printing Corporation and the shares held by the members of of Purnell and Sons Ltd. became shares in The British Printing Corporation. As a result of the successful offer made to the holders of the Ordinary Shares in Hazell Sun Ltd., The British Printing Corporation Limited acquired the whole of the Ordinary Shares in Hazell Sun Limited, issuing in part exchange Ordinary Shares in The British Printing Corporation Limited. A new company bearing the well known name of Purnell and Sons Limited was formed and this Company has acquired as a going concern from The British Printing Corporation Limited the business, assets and liabilities of the former Purnell and Sons Limited, issuing to the vendor company shares of the new Purnell and Sons Limited. This ensures the continuance of the two Groups of Purnell and Sons Limited and Hazell Sun Limited with The British Printing Corporation Limited as the Holding Company.

The merger of the two Groups as The British Printing Corporation Ltd. brought together the following companies under one management:

		Floor Space Sq. ft.	Freehold or Leasehold	Site Area Acres
A	HAZELL SUN GROUP			
1	Offset Litho Printers Chromoworks Ltd. Wigman Road, Nottingham.	59,000	L.99 from 24 .6 . 54	3
		Floor Space Sq. Ft.	Freehold or Leasehold	Site Area Acres
2	Web offset Printers Hazells Offset Ltd. Leigh Road Slough	73,700	L. Short'72	2.79
3	Offices Hazell Sun Ltd. 44 Great Queen Str. London W.C.2	16,800	L. 80 from 25 . 12. 57	3,700 .Sq, Ft.
4	Printers and Binders Hazell Watson & Viney Ltd. Aylesbury Bucks.	333,800	F	34.35

		Floor Space Sq. Ft.	Freehold or Leasehold	Site Area Acres
5	Social Club Britannia Street Aylesbury Bucks	9,240	F	0.47
6	Letterpress Printers Keliher, Hudson & Kearns 17 Hatfields London SE 1	45,000	L From 25. 3. 55	0.55
7	11 Theed Street London SE 1	9,400	L. 51 yrs. From 25. 3. 52	0.18
8	82 Southampton Drive London WC 2	800 (Shop)	L 13 yrs. From 25. 3. 63	-
9	2 Shops/Offices 111/115 Kingsway London WC 2	3,150	L. 63 yrs. From 24. 6. 21	-
10	Letterpress Printers Sidney Press Ltd. Sidney Road Bedford	29,850	F	1.26
11	Photogravure/Letterpress Printers. Sun Printers Ltd. Whippendale Road Watford Herts.	524,000	F	14.83
11a	Whippendale Road Watford Herts.	142,570	L. 99 yrs. from 25. 12. 53	13.16
12	Sports Ground Cassiobury Drive Watford Herts.		F	27.76

13   <u>Offset Litho</u>
<u>Carton Makers.</u>
Taylowe Ltd.   159,250   F   7.97
Malvern Road,
Furze Platt,
Maidenhead Berks.

B   <u>PURNELL GROUP</u>

1   <u>Paper Maker</u>
The Barrow Paper Mills Ltd.
Barrow-in-Furness
Lancs.   271750   F   24.7

2   <u>Newspapers/Printers</u>
Bird Bros. Ltd
Basingstoke, Hants.   7,750   F   0.18

3   <u>Periodical Publishers</u>
Bugle Press Ltd.
Noel Street,   1,400
London W 1   4,250   F   Sq. Ft.

4   <u>Newspapers/Printers</u>
Clare Son & Co Ltd.
Wells, Somerset.   19,850   F   0.66

	Floor Space Sq. Ft.	Freehold or Leasehold	Site Area Acres

5   <u>Point of sale Printers</u>
Henry Hildersly   46,000   F   0.67
Shackwell Lane
London E8

69 Heatherly St.   4,300
London E5   3,700   F   Sq. Ft.

73 Middle St.   2,400
Brighton   3,750   F   Sq. Ft.

6   <u>Bookbinders</u>
Key & Whiting Ltd.
Shaftesbury Road

		Floor Space Sq. Ft.	Freehold or Leasehold	Site Area Acres
	Edmonton London N18	19,100	F	0.965
	Harcourt Works Canonby Villas London N1	28,700	L	0.45
7	Bookbinders Nevett Ltd. The Hyde Colindale LondonNW9	65,150	F	2.35
8	Photogravure & General Printers Clarke & Sherwell Ltd. Kingsthorpe Road, Northampton	Not Available		
9	Printers Cox & Sharland 362 Spring Road, Southampton	N/A		
10	Paper Converters & Printers Cumberland Paper Company	N/A		
11	Paper Converters Cross Paperware Ltd. Dunstable, Beds.	N/A		
12	Label Printers Fell & Briant Ltd. Wallington Surrey	N/A		
13	Newspapers & Printing Gale & Polden Ltd. Aldershot Hants.	N/A		

Edinburgh Road,
Portsmouth Hants.   N/A

Guildford Road
Farnham, Surrey   N/A

95 High Street
Camberly, Surrey.   N/A

14   Printers
     John Drew (Printers) Ltd.
     Sebastopol Road
     Aldershot, Hants.   N/A

15   Printers
     F. A. Clements (Chatham) Ltd.
     High Street,
     Chatham   N/A

     40/42 Connaught Road
     Chatham   N/A

		Floor Space Sq. Ft.	Freehold or Leasehold	Site Area Acres
16	Printers E.D. Paine (Printing) Ltd. 28/36 Portland Road Worthing	N/A		
17	Process Engravers Nickeloid Ltd. 164 Union Street, London SE 1	43,000	L	0.21
18	Printers & Publishers Purnell & Sons Ltd. Paulton, Somerset	674,250	F	59.39
	Edwards Factory Paulton	12,200	F	0.47

Norton Hill

		Floor Space Sq. Ft.	Freehold or Leasehold	Site Area Acres
	Midsomer Norton Gulf House (3rd. Floor)	183,300	F	48.09
	2 Portman Street London W1	16,000	L 10 yrs. From 1962	-
	37 Hertford Street, London W1	3,650	L 52 yrs, From 1963	1,650 Sq. Ft.
19	Raphael Tuck Ltd. Paulton House, 8 Sheperdess Walk London N1	17,150	L 99 yrs. From1954	5,350 Sq. Ft.
	Pound Street Warminster	50,350	F	1.96
20	Reynolds Cards 10a Burnett Street, London SE 11	3,120	F	2,000 Sq. Ft.
21	Rishton Paper Mills Rishton Blackburn Lancs.	122,150 37,200	L F	17,83 1.71

		Floor Space Sq. Ft.	Freehold or Leasehold	Site Area Acres
22	Photogravure Printers L. T. A. Robinson Cranmer Road, London SW 9	64,450	L 24 yrs. From 1949	1,31
23	R. Somerville & Co. Ltd. Creech Paper Mills, Creech St. Michael, Taunton Somerset	67,250	F	5.3
24	Printers Waterlow & Sons Ltd. Waterlow House, Worship Street, London EC 2	109,300	F	0.80

		Floor Space Sq. Ft.	Freehold or Leasehold	Site Area Acres
25	Cheque Factory Vandy Street, London EC 2	40,000	F	0.22
26	11/16 Snowden Street London EC 2	4,350	F	0.32
27	Garage 28 Scrutton Street, London EC 2	5,200	F	0.13
28	Offices/Shops Blomfield House, 85/86 London Wall, London EC 2	33,000	L 21 yrs. From 1964	0.21
29	Printing (Radio Times) Twyford Abbey Road, Park Royal, London NW 10	110,800	L 42 yrs. From 1952	3.08
30	Printers & Binders Waterlow & Sons Ltd. George Street, Dunstable, Beds	394,000	F	14.21
31	Diary Production Seander Works Mary Street, Hyde, Cheshire	36,400	F	0.96
32	Radio Times Peel Park Place East Kilbride, Lanarkshire, Scotland	100,250	L. 40 yrs. From 1956	6.58
33	Sports Ground			

		Space Sq. Ft.	Freehold Leasehold	Acres
	High Street North, Dunstable, Beds		F	9.92
34	Sports Ground Chingford Road, Walthamstow, London E 17		F	6.76
35	Shop 109 The Headrow, Leeds	1,500	L. 10 yrs. From 1958	-
36	Offices Fourth Floor Century Buildings, 31 North John Street, Liverpool	375	L. 5 yrs. From 1961	-
37	<u>Stationery Printers</u> Harold Wesley Ltd. Acton Lane, London NW 10	222,400	F	8.57
38	Harley Mills Burton-on-Trent, Staffs.	53,000	F	1.19

39   Chain Libraries Ltd.

This business comprised six freehold properties and 33 leasehold premises, mainly shops, spread throughout England and Wales. The total valuation in 1964 was £246,825 the most expensive freehold shop being £30,000 in Boscombe, Hants.

The total valuation, carried out by Leopold Farmer & Sons, of The British Printing Corporation, as at 31st. December 1964, was as follows:

a)	Purnell Group Companies	£8,502,800
b)	Hazell Sun Group Companies	£5,646,550
c)	Chain Libraries	£ 246,825

All agricultural and residential properties were excluded from the above valuations.

On March 22nd. 1965 a schedule of Directors remuneration was produced at a Board meeting. The Hazell Sun Group Directors were angry and upset about the schedule's content for the following reasons given in a letter to the shareholders of The British Printing Corporation. Sir Geoffrey Crowther, Mr. Elliot Viney, Mr. Max Rayne and Mr. Leslie White signed the letter.

"The schedule showed that Mr. Harvey had a service agreement with the Company until December 31 1970, under which he claimed to be entitled to total remuneration in respect of 1964 to an amount of £270,000 which was approximately double that he had received in 1963. The Directors were further informed that his agreement entitled Mr. Harvey to a commission of 4% on trading profits of the Company (not only before taxation but also before interest) up to £20,000 and of 8% thereafter (without limit)

Since Hazell Sun Ltd. had become a subsidiary of BPC (formerly Purnell & sons Ltd.) the 8% commission had been applied to the profit of the whole of the Hazell Sun Group, without any deduction for interest on the money borrowed for the acquisition of these profits".

"At no time in the course of the merger negotiations had there been any disclosure to us or the shareholders of either company that one effect of the merger would be to divert a further sum of approximately £125,000 a year from the profits to Mr. Harvey's personal income."

"In addition to this commission, Mr Harvey draws expenses, the scope of which can be inferred from the fact that the portion of these expenses which the Revenue disallowed amounted to £98, 227 over seven years."

"In our opinion for any individual to claim from a public company of the size of BPC as remuneration for services in a single year a sum of money even approaching £270,000 (which is over 5% of the ordinary capital in issue at the end of the year) is grotesque and ridiculous".

"Any director truly solicitous of the interests of the shareholders who found himself through the wording of an agreement apparently entitled to any such sum would promptly waive the greater part of it ".

"When two of us put this point to him in the course of a discussion early in May 1965, the most Mr. Harvey would concede was that he would re-examine the position to see if there was any reduction that could be made 'without damage to his interests' by which he made it clear that he meant without any substantial reduction in the net benefit to him, especially in respect of pension benefit".

"He gave no sign of any willingness to renegotiate the agreement.

On May 19th. 1965 we then learned for the first time, to our astonishment, that between the date when the agreement for the merger and the formation of BPC had become effective, i.e. February 6th. 1964, and the date of the first meeting of the new board on March 12th. 1964, new service agreements had been given under the seal of Purnell & Sons Ltd. to the four Purnell Directors on the board of BPC. These are named as Mr. Wilfred Harvey, Mr Eric Harvey, Mr. J. C. Gibbs and Mr. S. V. Wilshire. Nothing had been said to us about these new service agreements at the first board meeting on March 12th. 1964".

"Mr. Wilfred Harvey's supplementary agreement contained a preliminary recital with regard to the expansion of the company's business. It then prolonged Mr. Harvey's terms of service as Managing Director to December 31st. 1970, an extension of three and a half years. Finally it provided that if Mr. Harvey ceased to be a Director of the Company 'for any reason other than retirement under clause 4 ' (there is in fact no clause 4), he was to be employed as Joint General Manger and Joint Sales Manager and to continue to receive the same salary and commission to which he was entitled as Managing Director".

'Such a transaction put through as it was without any prior reference o the Directors of Hazell Sun, and without disclosure to us when we oined the Board of BPC, must destroy all trust".

'The clause appointing him General Manager with the same emoluments, should he cease to be a Director, is in our view a wholly unjustified exercise of the Boards powers".

'But even this is not the whole of the unsatisfactory situation that we have had to meet. From the inception of the proposed merged corporation we have pressed for the reorganisation which was needed if the full benefits of the merger were to be reaped. There was (and is) scope for great economies through rationalisation. In short, the corporation should be effectively organised".

'Proposals on these lines, made by us, have been resisted or ignored by Mr. Harvey. We have learned that his manner of organisation is that everyone should report directly and exclusively to him. This reporting is not usually done at meetings so far as we can ascertain, few board meetings are held on the Purnell side of BPC: certainly we have never seen minutes of any".

"Indeed it is a rare thing for Mr. Harvey to put anything on paper. He prefers to direct personal and oral instructions to each of his subordinates separately. We do not believe that this is the way in which a large group of companies can be suitably administered even by a man of Mr. Harvey's industry and energy".

"Even if it were right for BPC to be run this way, it is necessary to recognise the fact that Mr. Harvey is in his 68th. year. He has not given any indication of when he proposes to retire and resents any discussion of the desirability of ensuring a proper succession".

On future policy for The British Printing Corporation, the letter tells shareholders that if resolutions are approved:

"We shall ask the Board to remove Mr. Harvey from all his other offices in the group. When this has been done we shall seek to appoint an independent Chairman of public standing and to restore the balance on the Board by appointing another Purnell representative We shall set about creating a management structure appropriate to the needs of this large public company, in which we shall do our best to secure the co-operation of the Purnell Directors. The elimination of extravagant management expenditure and the institution of improved methods of administration cannot fail to be of substantive benefit to the profits of the Corporation".

This letter was also printed in the National Press.

Shareholders were circulated on July 30th. 1965 with the statement that an agreed settlement had been reached in the dispute between the groups of Directors of BPC, providing, *inter alia*, for the retirement of Mr. W. Harvey and for an invitation to be extended to an outside person to become Chairman of the Corporation.

The Annual General Meeting of The British Printing Corporation was held at the Connaught Rooms, Great Queen Street, London WC 2 on Thursday 23rd. December 1965.

In the Report and Accounts Submitted to the shareholders prior to the meeting, the shareholders were to be asked to approve the changes in the composition of the Board as follows:

CHAIRMAN   Sir Walter Worboys

VICE CHAIRMAN   C. E. M.Hardie, CBE, FCA

        Sir Geoffrey Crowther
        J. C. Gibbs
        E. R. H. Harvey, MC, MA, BCL
        P. Lavington
        Max Rayne
        Elliott Viney

L. G. White
S. V. Wilshire

JOINT SECRETARIES

Bertram Clarke, FCA
E. A. Corp, FCA

The Report of the Directors stated that, " Since the last Annual General Meeting Mr. W. Harvey has retired from his office as Chairman and Managing Director of the Company and under the provisions of Article 110 of the Company's Articles of Association, the Directors have appointed Sir Walter Worboys, and Mr. C. E. M. Hardie whom they have elected Chairman and Vice Chairman respectively and Mr. P. Lavington as additional Directors of the Company".

In the same Report and Accounts the Joint Auditors, Cooper Bros. & Co. and Curtis, Jenkins, Cornwell & Co., added an appendix on page 14, as follows;

"To the Members of Purnell & Sons Limited. The balance sheet of the company is in agreement with the books.

The company, by an agreement dated 30th. December 1964, purchased as from the close of business on 31st. December 1963, the whole of the undertaking and business (excluding the shares in Hazell Sun Limited and certain liabilities) of its parent company, the former Purnell & Sons Ltd., now The British Printing Corporation Limited.

It has been the practice in the Purnell Group for many years to transfer the cost of investments, after acquisition by the parent company, to the wholly owned subsidiary company, Paulton Holdings Limited, and this cost is represented in the balance sheet of the company under the heading 'Investment and advance to subsidiary company, Paulton Holdings Limited' which is stated at £10,337,564.

As a result of information, which became available in July 1965, we have enquired into the circumstances of the acquisition of certain subsidiary companies and trade investments over a number of years and the true position with regard to a number of these transactions does not appear to us to be reflected in the books. In particular, we are not satisfied (a) that the accounts relative to certain of the transactions with Mr. Wilfred Harvey, the former chairman and managing director, as written up in the company's books, correctly reflect the position as at 31st.December 1964 (b) that the accounts showing no amount as a loan to a director in the balance sheets of the company or its subsidiary Paulton Holdings Limited are correct (c) that the amounts shown in the balance sheet as due from Paulton Holdings Limited are correct (d) that the purchase price entered in the books for some of the acquisitions are correct.

It is not appropriate in a report of this nature to give such details as we have of the many transactions about which we are not satisfied that the true position is recorded in the books, but, by way of example, we mention that in the case of the acquisition of one subsidiary the price recorded as paid by the company was £365,000, despite the fact that the subsidiary had reported to its shareholders that an offer had been received on behalf of the company at a price per share which would have resulted in a total purchase price of £76,669 and despite the fact that the total purchase price receivable by the former shareholders as disclosed in the transfers was in fact £76,669. We have been informed that Mr. Wilfred Harvey was interested in this transaction and we have also been informed by some other members of the board that they were aware that Mr. Harvey was interested, but we have received no satisfactory explanation why the purchase price recorded as paid by the company exceeded by £288,331 the price said to have been received by the former shareholders.

Acquisitions and disposals of certain other assets of the company and its subsidiary companies are still under detailed examination and adjustments to the accounts may be necessary in due course.

The consolidated accounts incorporate figures in respect of certain subsidiary companies, which have not been audited by us.

In our opinion, for the reasons given above, the accounts do not comply with the Companies Act, 1948, and we are not satisfied that they give a true and fair view of the state of affairs and the profit of the company and the group. Despite repeated requests we have not obtained the information and explanations we require and, in our opinion, the books have not been properly kept.

Wilfred Harvey retired on the 31st. October 1965.

At the Annual General Meeting 0n the 23rd December 1965, held in the Grand Hall of the Connaught Rooms in London, some 500 shareholders attended to learn more about a writ that had been issued against Wilfred Harvey claiming recovery of £288,000.

Sir Walter Worboys presided as Chairman and was immediately challenged as to whether he was 'the right and proper person' to preside at this meeting. After speaking with his legal adviser, Sir Walter said "Yes I am the proper person to conduct this meeting".

In his opening address Sir Walter Worboys said " We have already instituted proceedings against Mr. Wilfred Harvey in respect of the Chain Libraries transaction, which is the transaction referred to in the appendix to the report of the auditors".

During discussions on the matter, Mr. Parsons, a shareholder, asked for details of the writ. Mr. J. H. Thompson, the legal adviser for BPC replied, "It is a civil writ claiming the repayment to the company of £288,000 the difference referred to in the report. It makes certain alternative claims in addition, such as damages and in respect of negligence. It is quite a complicated document, but basically it is for the recovery of £288,000".

During the meeting, Mr. E. R. H. Harvey and Mr. Mr. J. C. Gibbs, who were retiring by rotation, did not offer themselves for re-election.

Mr. Peter Lavington, who had joined the board in June 1965, also did not seeking re-election. Mr. Stanley Victor Wilshire also resigned from the parent board at the end of the meeting.

Mr. Parsons, a shareholder asked another question, "As there are now only two practical printers, Mr. L. G. White and Mr. Elliott Viney left on the Board, what are you going to do about that?".

Sir Walter replied that the Directors were working towards a reconstruction of the Board. He hoped that members would allow a new Chairman a little bit longer than the six or seven weeks he had been with the company to determine what the composition of that Board should be.

In May 1966 the appointments to the Board were announced, to become effective from the 1st. July 1965, as follows:

Mr. S. V. Bishop	Managing Director
Mr. John Pollock	Commercial Director
Sir Maurice Dean	Personnel Director
Mr. J. M. Pickhard	Finance Director
Mr. L. G. White	Vice- Chairman BPC
Mr. Robert Paterson	Managing Director of Purnell & Sons Ltd. (appointed Feb.'66).

Mr Peter Robinson and Mr. Gilbert Smith have been appointed Associate Directors and if the annual general meeting approve the alterations to article 88, it is our intention to appoint them full Directors.

So, for the first time since 1924, when Wilfred Harvey joined Purnells, 41 years ago, the Paulton factory was without its long standing governor, and this at a time when there were large expansion developments taking place in the packaging, photogravure and web-offset departments. Fortunately for Purnells, the new Managing Director, Robert Paterson, was a man of great leadership qualities and the plans for Paulton went ahead steadily, despite the upheavals that had taken place at main board level. Co-operation and help between the BPC factories had been good at factory and departmental level since the merger, and continued to be so.

Mr. Paterson, the new Managing Director of Purnells, had a long association with the printing trade. He had joined the sales staff of J.J. Keliher in 1925 and became a Director in 1935 at the age of 27. The following year he became a Director of Tonbridge Printers.

In 1939 J.J. Keliher merged with Hudson and Kearns, the new company taking the name of Keliher, Hudson and Kearns Ltd. who became part of BPC letterpress division in the 1960's. In 1950 Keliher, Hudson and Kearns had been taken over by Illustrated Newspapers. In 1952 Mr. Paterson became Managing Director of Keliher, Hudson and Kearns and in the same year he was elected to the Board of Michael Joseph, the publishers. In 1953 he joined the Board of Beric Press and in 1961 the Board of Illustrated Newspapers.

He became Chairman of Keliher, Hudson and Kearns in 1963. Owing to the takeover of Illustrated Newspapers in 1961, by the Thomson Organisation, some of his directorships lapsed.

Clifford J. Purnell, the long retired son of the founder of the business, and past Chairman of the Company from 1935, was still living in the house where he was born at Park Corner Paulton. He must have been saddened by the events that had overtaken Wilfred Harvey, the man he once called a genius, but pleased that no court of law ever found Wilfred Harvey guilty of any misdemeanour.

In the 1970 Report and Accounts, note 22 reads: During the year a settlement was reached in respect of legal proceedings commenced in 1966 in relation to a number of transactions entered into by Purnell & sons Ltd. and its then subsidiary, Paulton Holdings Limited, during the year ending 31st. December 1965 and previous years in which a former Director was concerned. A net sum of £240.000 was received which is shown under exceptional items in the Profit and Loss Account.

In 1971, the alleged fraud cases against Wilfred Harvey were dropped due to his deteriorating health and advancing years, he was now 73 years old.

The corporation profit, after taxation, for the 1960's was:

1960	£377,948
1961	£688,534
1962	£703,955
1963	£879,899
1964	£1,179,073
1965	£775,813
1966	£1,081,716
1967	£1,584,119
1968	£1,998,000
1969	£465,000

The figures for 1966 to 1969 are from the seven-year financial summary (1966-1972) issued as a Report of the Directors in 1973, whereas the 1960 to 1965 results are from the Purnell Report and Accounts.

In 1967 several BPC companies were sold off. These included Galleon Printers Ltd, Kayebon Press Ltd., Chain Libraries, Chandler (Print) Ltd., and the Norton Hill factory of Purnells, the packaging business, called Runprint Ltd.

The envelope manufacturing department of Runprint was retained and moved back to the main factory at Paulton, where it continued under the successive departmental management of Cyril Dyer, Ian Wilcox and Wendy Gregory.

The envelope department continued manufacturing long after the book printing and binding departments closed down.

GREETINGS TELEGRAM **GPO**

6011 AP8 8.0 BUCKINGHAM PALACE OHMS 35 ALLPURPOSE

MR CLIFFORD JOHN PURNELL PARK CORNER PAULTON

BRISTOL SOMERSET =

THE QUEEN IS MUCH INTERESTED TO HEAR THAT YOU

RE CELEBRATING YOUR ONE HUNDREDTH BIRTHDAY

AND SENDS YOU WARM CONGRATULATIONS AND GOOD

WISHES = PRIVATE SECRETARY +

A cause for the Company to cheer up and celebrate was Clifford Purnells 100th. Birthday on the 3rd. March 1965. Not too many of these telegrams are seen these days, Clifford Purnell lived to attain the age of 106 years ..

.

Clifford Purnell's 100th. birthday celebration. On this occasion, a visit from the ladies of the bindery.

Wilfred Harvey's involvement with Purnell had now ceased and he and his wife settled into retirement, in the gatehouse of The Chase at Winsley, now owned by his daughter Betty and her husband Peter Lavington.

Wilfred Harvey had bought The Chase at Winsley, the former home of Admiral Sir Richard Poore an ADC to Edward VII, in1935. In 1946 he bought a town house in London, No.1 Orme Square, Bayswater, former home of Lord May, secretary of the Prudential. His increasing involvement with the London based businesses made this necessary.

Horse breeding and racing became a family interest for the Harvey family. In 1947 he bought the Sandwich Stud of 150 acres near Newmarket from the Earl of Roseberry and Jack Jarvis the trainer.

The manager of his stud was Mr. Robert Waugh, and at one time it was reckoned that he owned over a 100 horses, of which two had notable victories. Star King won the 1948 Gimcrack Stakes at York and Supertello won the Ascot Gold Cup in 1950. Both Mrs. Harvey and her daughter Betty owned and raced horses in their own racing colours. In 1950 Wilfred Harvey sold his stud to the Aga Khan and Aly Khan, together with over 50 of his best stock, in a package said to be worth £170,000. After this sale, Wilfred Harvey's the interest in horses diminished for a few years until the early 1960's when he started buying again, one of these, bought at Deauville, was Niksar, which won the 2,000 Guineas and was later sold for 48,000 Guineas.

Looking back over the period when Wilfred Harvey was Chairman of Purnells, he achieved an enormously successful record for returning profits and improving the balance sheet of the company year after year.

Yes, he was autocratic, right from the onset; his reasons for this appear to be his single-minded insistence on secrecy with business deals, especially takeovers. The first instance of this is seen in the founding of the Macdonald publishing company and later when the company bought local farmland, he used his daughter's married name on the deeds to Downs Farm in Paulton. He needed people with him that he could trust; inevitably this led to nepotism as many of his family joined him at Purnells.

He also practiced what he preached, and he emphasised at every opportunity, that the directors should be full time working for the business, no part time directorships to take one's eye off of the main business.

His main failing perhaps was not to notice that as the company rapidly grew in the 1960's, that it was becoming very complicated and needed a division of responsibilities and some management succession planning at top board level.

Clifford Purnell reading the Queen's telegram, on his 100th. Birthday, with Eric Harvey looking over his shoulder.

. On Mr. Purnell's subsequent birthdays he kept open house at Park Corner and received many visits from the staff from across the road.

This was the last birthday photograph taken of Clifford Purnell, he was 106 years old and looking spruce with his traditional buttonhole. Sadly he died on the 8th. May 1971. All his life Clifford Purnell remained a vegetarian, a total abstainer, a non-smoker, and a bachelor. Being a devout Christian, he was passionately involved with the local Central Methodist Church.

The whole of the Purnell's factory came to a stand still for one hour on the afternoon of the funeral on May 13th. most of the 2,000 employees attended the funeral.

THE HISTORY OF PURNELL & SONS LTD.

The management structure at Paulton, as at April 1ˢᵗ. 1969, was defined as there being four areas of responsibility, reporting to Robert Paterson as follows:

	Managing Director	Robert Paterson
1)	Director Gravure Division	Peter Lavington
2)	Director Main Division	Bill Harvey
3)	Administrative Director & General Manager	Eric Harvey
4)	Company Secretary & Finance Director	David Bailey

The above five directors represented the senior management of the Paulton factory, including Bristol Photo Engraving, Western Ink, Purnell & Sons, and R. Somerville & Co.

The Gravure Division's management structure was :

1)	Director Gravure Division	Peter Lavington
2)	Deputy Manager	Peter Williams
	Reporting to Peter Williams were eight managers and staff	

3)	Ink Factory	L. C. Perry
	Engineering	D. Cornish
	Projects	D.Dereham
	BPE Manager	Eric Bugden
	Printing	Charles Carpenter
	Production Planning	Alan Grainger
	Warehouse	Brian Shales
	Costing & Admin.	R. Wallis

Eric Bugden was the manager responsible for scanning, studio, retouching, planning, carbon, etching, engraving and copper plating.

The Main Division's management structure was :

1)   Director Main Division   Bill Harvey

2)   Deputy Works Manager   Donald McIntosh
         Reporting directly to Donald McIntosh were 14 managers and staff.

3)   Chief Engineer   Maurice Harvey
         Material QC & Chemist   H. Fowler
         Organisation& Methods   D. Wilson

4)   Production Control   Ken Bateson
         Composing Dept.   Frank Woodland
         Envelope Dept.   Cyril Dyer
         Litho Dept.   Bob Wilshire
         Web Offset   Frank Sullivan
         Bindery   Bert Alderton
         Letterpress   Stan Evans
         Folding Room   Alf Carey
         Warehouse Sheets   L.(Mick) Hewish
         Warehouse (finished)   E. Salvidge
         Despatch   Stan Cottle

5)   Deputy Binding Manager   Arthur Spackman

   Also reporting directly to Bill Harvey were:

         Direct Mail Manager   R. Morgan
         Service Centre Manager   Don Milverton
         Western Ink Gen. Manager Les Mathews

   The Western Ink Works Manager was Bill Dean reporting to Les Mathews.

The Administration and General Management Director, Eric Harvey had two important staff members reporting to him:

Personnel Manager	Arthur Cornish
Training Officer	J. G. Morgan

The Company Secretary and Financial Director, David Bailey, had the following reporting to him:

Chief Buyer	Laurie Carter
Financial Accountant	J. N. Moss
Management Accountant	John Thomson
Associate Companies	Eddie Parker

These positions were taken at a fixed point in time, April 1st. 1969, and of course quite a few changed in the future through transfers, promotions and retirements.

Laurie Carter, the Chief Buyer for Purnells had a son Tim who was also on the staff. Tim had joined Purnells in 1960 as a trainee and subsequently moved to the Sommerville paper mill in1965 as assistant manager. He became the General Manager in 1966 and was elected to the board of R. Somerville & Co. Ltd. in 1970. Sadly Tim was killed in a road accident in 1973 at an age of 33 years, a great waste of a Paulton born man of talent.

An aerial view of the new Purnell Gravure Hall, Boiler House and Ink Factory.

It is interesting to see just how much of BPC's profit was generated by Purnells in the 1960's and below is given a comparison between the final accounts of a) BPC b) Purnell Group and c) Purnell & Sons Ltd. for the year 1969.

	BPC £'000	Purnell Group £'000	Purnell & Sons Ltd. £'000
Outside Sales	£69,387	£12,114	£5,355
Group Sales	£8,250	£4,997	£3,230
	£77,637	£17,111	£8,585
Trading Profit Excluding Sun & ILSC	4,749	2,807	2,052
Sun Loss	(175)	-	-
	4,574	2,807	2,052
Interest Charges P &PG @7% of BPC	1,525	525	330
	3,049	2,282	1,722
Net Profit Provision against ILSC	1,431	836	793
Pre-tax Profit	1,618	1,446	929

178

CHAPTER TEN

THE NEW REGIME

Let us take a look at the new men at the head of The British Printing Corporation, beginning with the Chairman.

Sir Walter Worboys was 65 years old, when asked to join BPC; he had been Chairman and Managing Director of BTR Industries Ltd. since 1960. Among his other directorships are those of the Westminster Bank Ltd., Associated Portland Cement Manufacturers Ltd. and The Forestal Land, Timber and Railways Co. Ltd.

Sir Walter Worboys was born in Australia and educated at the university of Western Australia and Lincoln College Oxford. He was a director of ICI from 1948 to 1959 and also Chairman of the Council of Industrial Design from 1953 to 1960.

It should be remembered that BPC had very large debts, and its principle creditor was the Westminster Bank and as a director of that bank, he was entreated, after much persuasion, to occupy the vacant chair at BPC.

Sir Walter's immediate task was to find and build a corporate team of top executives to direct the corporation. This was done by personal contact and recommendation largely by Sir Walter and Charles Hardie the new Vice Chairman of BPC.

Charles E. M. Hardie, the new Vice-Chairman of BPC, was a Chartered Accountant of Dixon, Wilson, Tubbs and Gillet, Chartered Accountants and was the financial adviser to BPC. Mr Hardie was 55 years old and was the Chairman of Metropolitan Estates and Property Corporation, and of Radio Rentals Ltd., Deputy Chairman of BOAC, the Vokes Group Ltd., NAFFI, and a Director of several other companies, including the Anglo-Portugese Bank Ltd, Bowmakers Ltd. Drages Ltd. and Hallmark Cards (Great Britain) Ltd.

Mr. S. V. Bishop was the new Managing Director of BPC. After a search through the printing industry to find an executive, capable of running a large corporation and not succeeding, the Massey-Ferguson group supplied the answer with a director from their British subsidiary, Perkins, the diesel engine makers, in the form of Mr. Bishop. Mr. Bishop had been involved in reorganising the Massey- Ferguson's operating structure, a task that was needed urgently at BPC.

One of the useful things introduced by Mr. Bishop, was establishing the BPC Newsletter, which enabled senior executives to know what their colleagues were doing throughout the corporation.

Mr. Bishop resigned from his appointments as deputy chairman and joint managing director of BPC and also his appointment as chairman of International Learning Systems Corporation, according to a BPC announcement on June 1st. 1970. His services would continue to be available to BPC on a consultative basis. The board paid tribute to Mr. Bishop's contribution to the corporation from when he joined BPC in July 1966.

Robert Paterson the new director in charge of Purnells at Paulton, had been the Managing Director of Keliher Hudson and Kearns. Mr. Paterson had held directorships of: Tonbridge Printers, Michael Joseph the publishers,Beric Press and Illustrated Newspapers. He was said to have been a man of great leadership qualities and he was appointed a Vice Chairman of the Corporation in January 1969.

Mr. Lesley White was already a director of BPC from the Hazell Sun Group, since 1964 and is Vice Chairman of BPC since May 1966. He joined Hazell Watson & Viney in 1922. From1946 to 1952 he was manager of Hazells Long Acre works, became a director and was Managing Director of Sidney Press Bedford. In 1952 he became Production Director of Sun Printers, Watford, then Managing Director and then Chairman of the company. Mr. White was appointed deputy chairman of Hazell Sun in 1964 and a director of BPC,

Sir Maurice Dean who was Permanent Secretary at the Ministry of Technology and upon his retirement from the civil service joined BPC as Personnel Director in1966. He became supervising director of the Sun Group in July 1968.

Sir Maurice became a KCMG in 1949 and a KCB in1957. He had joined the Civil Service, from Cambridge in 1928, and served in the Air Ministry, the control office for Germany and Austria, the Foreign Office, the Ministry of Defence, the Treasury and the Board of Trade.

Michael Pickhard who was recruited under the auspices of Charles Hardie as Financial Controller, became the Financial Director of BPC. On the 27th. March 1968, BPC published a press statement that Mr. Pickhard had resigned as an executive member of the board effective from the 30th.June 1968, in order to take up the managing directorship of Trust Houses Ltd. Mr. Pickhard remains as a non-executive director

John Pollock, who was Assistant General Manager of "The Times" joined BPC as Commercial Manager. After war service John Pollock joined St. Clements Press, becoming City Manager. In 1950 he joined the Readers Digest as Production Manager. He started the Dutch edition of Reader's digest in1957.
In 1959 he became assistant to the general manager of international editions in the USA. He also worked for Newsweek as Promotions Director of the Atlantic edition. He was appointed Publishing Director of BPC in 1967. BPC announced on March 19th. 1971 that Mr. Pollock was to leave the board of BPC on March 31st. with terms mutually agreed. Mr. Pollock's direct responsibilities for the Publishing Group had ceased in 1969.

Mr. Elliott Viney was already a board member from the Hazell Sun Group since 1964 and a member of the well-known printing family that is part of Hazell Watson & Viney Ltd. at Aylesbury, Cymmer, and Slough. He was manager of the Aylesbury factory from 1946 to 1959 and Chairman of Hazells from 1966 to 1967. In 1973 Mr. Viney was elected president of the British Federation of Master Printers.

Mr. Max Rayne was a major shareholder in BPC, through his company London Merchant Securities. In 1963 London Merchant Securities had acquired a substantial shareholding in the Hazell Sun Group from the International Publishing Corporation. Mr.Rayne sold his shareholding in BPC in 1968 and as a result resigned his directorship, thus ending a five-year relationship with the corporation.

Mr. Arnold Montague Alfred was appointed to the BPC board in January 1969 with a starting date of April 1969 and the position of Planning Director. His duties were to assist other directors in the preparation and co-ordination of the long-term plans of their Corporation. He had been with Courtalds since 1946 and was currently head of the economics department, co-ordinator of management services and a director of the Celon division.

Mr. Laurence Peterken joined the Corporation in February 1966 and succeeded Mr. Gilbert Smith as director in charge of the Waterlow Group. He joined AEI in1955, as assistant to the company secretary, became manager of Hotpoint's service division in 1961 and Hotpoint's commercial director in1963. He was educated at Harrow and at Cambridge where he took a 2nd.class Honours in Law.

Mr. Gilbert Smith was a printer, he started his career as in 1931 as an apprentice compositor with the Amalgamated Press at the age of 15. He went to India in 1937 as assistant superintendent of Thackers Press in Calcutta. In 1939 he joined Hunt Barnard in Aylesbury but war broke out and he left to go to Sandhurst and ended up in the 4th Tank Regiment. He was captured on the outskirts of Tobruk in 1942 and interned in Italy where he managed to escape and joined the Airborne Forces. After the war he joined Hazell Watson & Viney and became Technical Director in 1952. He was responsible for the installation of the Goss, letterpress, web, magazine press that printed the Reader's Digest magazine at Aylesbury for many years. In 1957 he was the director responsible for setting up at Slough, Hazells Offset Ltd., Britain's first heatset, web offset, plant

Mr. Richard Holme who was chief executive of BPC Publishing and before that BPC's publishing groups marketing director from April 1967. Previously he was the marketing director for Penguin books whom he had joined in 1965

Mr. Holme was educated at Oxford and then went to Unilever as a management trainee. During his six years there he specialised in marketing and became marketing director of Carrs of Carlisle, the biscuit producers. Mr. Holme became a BPC main board director on the 17th. December 1969 and Chairman of BPC Publishing. The BPC board announced on December 30th. 1969 that Mr. Holme and Mr. Galliner were to leave the Corporation following Publishing Group Losses of about £1,000,000 and stock write-offs of almost £1,750,000.

The losses were mainly due to weakened markets in Partwork Publications and, to a lesser degree, books.

Lord Kings Norton joined the board of BPC in October 1968, as a non-executive director. Lord Kings Norton, formerly Sir Harold Roxbee Cox was an engineer. He gained a first class Honours degree in mechanical engineering and trained with the Austin Motor Company. After war work at the Minisry of Aircraft Production, he became director of the National Gas Turbine Establishment in 1946 and in1948 was was appointed chief scientist of the ministry of Fuel and Power. He was Knighted in 1953. He became chairman of the Metal Box Company in 1961 and chairman of Berger, Jensen and Nicholson, paint manufacturers, in 1967. He was also chairman of Sidney-Barton the public relations consultancy. He was created a Life Peer in 1965.

Peter Robinson became a member of the BPC board in 1966, as supervising director of the Paper and Packaging Group. He was a Hazell Sun director and director of BPC's two companies in Canada. He joined Taylowe Ltd. at Maidenhead in 1954 as works manager, became managing director in 1963 and chairman in 1967.

Much was achieved by some of the new directors, but on the other hand, some very costly misjudgements in management took place, which had adverse financial results for the Corporation, that was already bearing high interest charges on large borrowings from the bank.

Back at Paulton, in 1965 and 1966, the factory was now being managed with the following team.

Mr. R. Paterson   Managing Director
Mr. S. V. Wilshire
Mr. E. R. H. Harvey
Mr. W. J. Harvey
Mr. P. Lavington
Mr. A. C. Grant
Mr. J. C. Gibbs

The departments, in 1965, were nearly all at technical transformation stages; for example, the composing department was still heavily into hot metal but had a Lino Film system, i.e. Keyboard and Photo-Unit working alongside the Monotype and Linotype hot metal machines. The Printing Department was also still heavily into letterpress, with eight 8Crown Perfecting presses, a Quad Royal Perfector, a Quad Demy Perfector, two Quad Demy Singles, one 8Crown Single (hand fed) and two Quad Crown Singles (hand fed). There was a 2 Colour Timson Rotary, 13, 2 Colour L & M flatbeds, one Miehle Horizontal Tandem, six Miehle Horizontals, nine Miehle Verticals and a Platen.

The ever-growing Offset Department, in 1965, had a single colour Harris (D/Medium) No. 214, a single colour Harris (Q/Demy) No. 217, two 2-Colour Harris (41 x 54) No's. 222 & 223, a 2-Colour Harris (23 x 36) No.224, a 2-Colour Roland (45 x 65) No.226, a 4-Colour Harris No.242, three 4-Colour Roland presses No's 246, 247, and 248, a 4-Colour Crabtree (44 x 64) No.249 and a 6-Colour Roland (39 x 59). There were two ATF web offset presses of 36" and 38" that had been installed from 1961.

The folding, wire stitching and cased bindery departments had increased in size and had introduced new processes to meet the demands of the printing departments. The binding of mail order catalogues was seasonal, taking up six weeks in June and July, then beginning again in December for six weeks. Over the years Purnells had become experts, not only in binding the various styles of catalogues, but in the complicated warehousing and progress chasing involved in obtaining from several printers, required quantities of specific sections, for several different catalogues, to be bound in their unique binding style, i.e. wire stitched, thread sewn or perfect bound.

The man who controlled this operation at Paulton for many years was Mr. W. J. Harvey, the son of Fred Harvey, and known to all as Bill Harvey. Bill Harvey became Joint Managing Director together with Peter Lavington on 1st. April 1970.

Three more appointments were made to the Purnell board in 1970. Arthur Cornish became Personnel Manager; Donald McIntosh became Works Manager and Peter Williams, Gravure manager.

Arthur Cornish was the personnel and technical officer for Purnells, becoming Personnel Director in 1970. Arthur's details are given elsewhere in this book. Arthur died in 1973 aged 65 years. His son David was an engineer in the Gravure department.

Donald McIntosh was apprenticed with the Stirling Observer. He worked for ten years at Sun Printers in Watford and joined Purnells in 1961. He established and managed a Cost System, and an Estimating Department before becoming Works Director and Managing Director. He was also the founder of the Purnell Study Group, a very useful and educational group for the development of managers and staff at Paulton.

Peter Williams began his career commissioning Electronic equipment for Crossfield. In 1959 he joined the Italian press manufacturing company of Cerutti as technical sales manager. He joined Purnells in 1964 as Gravure manager. He later became a director of BPE and then Sales Director of Purnell.

Purnells had installed at Paulton, in January 1965, an IBM-1440 computer, but computer technology was advancing so quickly at this time, that by 1968, when it became necessary to install a total management system, a more powerful and efficient computer was required. The computer was installed to improve Purnell Publishing efficiency and did so for the first five years. Eventually it developed into the following areas:

A)   BPC Publishing
1) Sales accounting, Stock Control Books, toys and games.
2) Sales accounting, stock recording Part-works.
3) Sales accounting, Stock recording Magazines.
4) Magazine & part-work subscriptions
5) Salaries.
6) Credit Control and Stock Valuation.

B)   The printing works
1) Wages & Salaries
2) Bought Ledger and raw material control.
3) Job Costing
4) Departmental operating costs.
5) Sales Ledger.
6) Production Planning

C)   Group Companies
1) Nickeloid; Wages & Salaries.
2) R. Somerville; Wages & Salaries.
3) Bristol Photo Engraving; Wages & Salaries.
4) Western Ink Co.; Wages & Salaries.

A new computer was ordered, a model IBM-360/30, for delivery in July 1968. The computer was delivered ahead of schedule on July the 8th. 1968 and a series of rigorous installation tests completed by the 29th. July. The transfer of improved versions of applications from the 1440 was completed by the year-end.

Brian Eatock, the second data processing manager since 1966, visited the Italian firm of Mondadori, in Verona and Milan, to study their computer systems as they were recognised as print industry leaders in production oriented computer systems.

At the same time BPC Publishers required a modern book storage and distribution centre, computer driven, to meet their requirements for the 1970's. To this end, was approved for construction, a 83,000 sq, ft warehouse and offices, to be constructed on the Paulton site by Ernest Ireland, the Bath contractors, for a sum of £330.000 plus an additional £130.000 for modern, movable, book storage racking and other equipment. Bill Harvey who chaired many meetings over the two-year planning period led this project team.

The manager of the book centre was to be Mr. Donald Milverton. The following photographs show the construction of the book centre Stage by stage.

Brian Eatock, far left, with the new IBM-360/30 computer in July 1968.

This photograph of the Book Centre site was taken on the 11th.June 1968. The residents in the cottages seen in the background complained, as the building gained height, that it was like living under a cliff.

This photo. was taken on the 21st. July 1968 from almost the same spot as the above one.

The 9th. August 1968, things are moving quickly in the summer months.

The 11th. November 1968, the steelwork goes up.;

December 9th. 1968 The dispatch area taking shape.

December 12th. 1968

April 25th. 1969

The first load of books arrives in April 1969, the company made sure that all systems were running smoothly before the official opening.

The official opening of the Book Service Centre on July 10th. 1970. Mr. B. Eatock is leading the guests through the motorised racking.

The order picking lifts in operation in 1970. The racks, five bays high, contained loose parcels or pallets of books and these could be closed up and opened at will to save on gangway access space.

Don Milverton, the Book Centre Manager, with Richard Holme, Chairman of BPC Publishing, studying an architectural model of the Service Centre, under the watchful eye of Clifford J. Purnell, behind them, son of the founder of Purnell & Sons.

At the official opening of the Book Centre 45 customers and Press representatives were present on July 10th. 1970. The chairman, Mr. Richard Holme, thanked all the guests for attending and then thanked the management, together with the Management Consultants, P. A. Limited, for the splendid job that they had done in designing and building such an efficient Book Centre. What had taken over two weeks in ordering and despatching books would now be done in three and a half days.

This early 1970's aerial photograph shows the Paulton factory site of Purnells Ltd. shortly after completion of the building of the Book Centre pictured at the extreme right of the photograph.

At the time of writing much has changed, the Book Centre has stood empty for a long time and the old boot factory, seen at the extreme left of the photograph, that belonged to the Flook and Butler families respectively, has been levelled and replaced with a housing estate.

The above picture illustrates very well the sloping nature of the site as it drops down towards the Cam brook. This slope helped the gravure factory building in getting the paper reel store and re-reeling facility housed beneath the gravure presses

The building of the book Service Centre, in 1970, was the last development to take place to date, and when one looks at the aerial photograph of 1970 and compares it to the one on page 20, one cannot fail to be impressed at what was achieved in 40 years.

CHAPTER ELEVEN

THE 1970'S

The 1970's did not begin well for the British Printing Corporation, the main difficulties centred on the Publishing Group, on part-works and reference books such as encyclopaedias to be more precise.

Purnells you will recall, put their first web-offset press into the Paulton factory in1961, an ATF press that was soon joined by another one. Purnells first published major part work, was printed by sheet fed litho, and was called "Knowledge". Comprising 216 parts in 18 volumes, in1961. Four reprints were subsequently run off in following years, and then a new edition was launched on December 1st. 1969, each part to sell at 2/6. Many other part-work titles were printed during the 1960's with varying degrees of success. The two ATF presses at Paulton were kept reasonably busy and under the management of Frank Sullivan became efficient and even won some awards for the quality of the product.

Among those responsible for Purnells and BPC's success in publishing part-works were Norman Marshall, the publisher and Patrick Cavendish, the Marketing Manager. In July 1967, these two gentlemen decided to leave BPC and start their own part-work business called Marshal Cavendish Ltd. John Pollock was to absorb Norman Marshall's duties and Richard Holme those of Patrick Cavendish.

In November 1967, John Pollock announced the appointment of Peter Galliner as Managing Director of BPC Publishing Ltd. Also in 1967, BPC began a joint venture with Pergamon Press, owned by Robert

Maxwell, by investing £1,100,000 in International Learning Systems Corporation, a 50% interest in a business that published encyclopaedias.

BPC and Pergamon Press announced in a joint press release on February 19th.1970, the termination of their equal partnership in International Learning Systems Corporation. The terms of the agreement were:

BPC will acquire immediately 1.6 million 10s. shares (40% of the issued capital) from Pergamon, and Pergamon will assign to BPC the balance currently due to Pergamon by ILSC on loan account of approximately £1,340,000 for an aggregate consideration of £200,001.

Pergamon will pay £175,000 to ILSC in full and final settlement of its profit warranty.

Pergamon will be released from and BPC will assume all liabilities in respect of guarantees, and other contingent liabilities of ILSC.

ILSC and Pergamon have settled all disputed transactions and other arrangements between the two companies.
BPC will have the right to buy Pergamon's remaining 10% holding. On its part Pergamon has the right to require BPC to buy these remaining shares.

The representatives of Pergamon on the board of ILSC are to resign.
The agreement is conditional on the approval by April 30th. 1970 of BPC's Debenture and Loan Stockholders to amendments to the terms of these stocks.

The statement continued: "The management and administration of ILSC has been reorganised in recent months and its business has been re-established on a footing which gives confidence for the future. There is, however, a need to provide considerable sums to finance the development of the company, for which BPC is making provision. The board of Pergamon consider that in its present circumstances

Pergamon is not in a position to raise sums of this order to maintain its equal partnership with BPC in ILSC. Pergamon therefore welcomes this opportunity for the restructuring of the partnership agreement offered by BPC, which will enable BPC to develop ILSC as a member of the BPC Group.

In a letter to share holders, the chairman, Mr. Hardie said: "In my letter of September19th. 1969, I told you that it was not possible at that time to make long-term arrangements for the operation of ILSC but that I believed it was right for BPC to be in the encyclopaedia business. We now believe that the management and procedures exist within this company to make the acquisition of the Pergamon share in ILSC a logical move for BPC. I believe that this move fits well into BPC's long-term plans to expand in the international publishing business. This brings to a close a long period of uncertainty."

On the15th.April 1970, an Extraordinary General Meeting was called and about 60 BPC shareholders attended at the Chartered Insurance Institute, E.C.2. Mr. Hardie announced that "There is no resolution in front of this meeting; it is simply a get together of shareholders - a thing that ought to be done more frequently by companies - to question the directors about a particular situation."

Pre-tax Profits (subject to ILSC trade account provisions) down £3.8 million to about £3 million.

Dividend cut from 17.5% to 12.5%

A write-off of £3,653,000 net on ILSC

Annual General Meeting not to be held until July 1970, because of the delay in auditing ILSC's accounts.

Mr. Hardie continued, that the board was very conscious that no proper figures or information about ILSC had been forthcoming. "It has been very frustrating for everybody", he said, "Such has been the state of preparation of accounts overseas and in this country that only last Friday afternoon was I able myself to get the basic figures for submission to this meeting."

He emphasised that 1970 would undoubtedly be a hard year and BPC was not anticipating any contributions from ILSC to its 1970 profits."Indeed there could be a small loss," he said. The BPC board announced on December 30th.1970, that the corporation would show a loss of around £1.5 million for 1970, following Publishing Group losses of £1 million and a write-off of almost £1.75 million of stocks, promotional and development costs. The board said it was unlikely to recommend any dividend on the ordinary share capital for 1970.

The announcement added that Richard Holme, a main board director and chairman of BPC Publishing, and Peter Galliner, vice-chairman (formerly managing director) of BPC publishing, were to leave the corporation.

The printing and binding of ILSC encyclopaedias was worth just over £1,500,000 in 1969, it kept several BPC factories busy.

In mid July 1971 the Department of Trade and Industry published a report by their inspectors who had conducted an investigation into the affairs of Pergamon Press and ILSC. The report contained parts that were critical of BPC and some of it's officers and being published just a week before BPC's Annual General Meeting caused some embarrassment that needed some denials and explanations in front of the share holders.

The following is the full text of the statement made by the chairman and Michael Pickard at the Annual General Meeting:

The chairman said:

Shareholders will be aware of the publication last week of the report of the inspectors appointed by the Department of trade and Industry to investigate the affairs of Pergamon and ILSC.

In view of the publicity which followed and of the fact that the report contains passages critical of your company and certain of it's officers, past and present, your directors wish to make it plain that:

1)   They are quite unable to accept the accuracy of certain of those passages;

2)   They were given no fair opportunity to meet the criticisms made in the report;

3)   Legal proceedings have been issued by your company challenging the validity of the report in respect of the passages complained of.

Mr. Pickard, in whom the board has complete confidence, has asked me to state that he repudiates the observations in the report critical of him.

Whilst it can now be seen that the decision to become involved in a 50/50 venture with Pergamon in which managerial control was not with us, was a serious mistake, my board has no doubt whatever as to the integrity of those concerned in these matters on behalf of your company. Having regard to the pending legal proceedings, shareholders will we hope, understand if at this stage I elaborate no further. But in general I would like to mention a point for your consideration:-

As already stated, your board made an error of judgement in going into partnership with Pergamon in ILSC. However, commercial decisions have to be made on the facts available at the time without the benefit of hindsight. At the time your board made its decision, Pergamon was seriously regarded by a large section of investment analysts, stock- brokers, financial journalists and merchant bankers as a company of repute, as is evidenced by the support given to its various ventures at that time. We ask to be judged solely on the basis of facts as then known to us.

Mr. Pickard said:-

A number of specific criticisms have been made by the inspectors about the actions I took in my capacity as finance director of BPC in the formation and first year's activities of ILSC. In view of both the remarks of the inspectors and the subsequent press comment I would like to make the following specific points:-

1)   I was unaware of a substantial proportion of the evidence given by Caxton and find that I am in complete disagreement on a number of vital issues.

   a) As finance director of BPC I was continually telling Caxton that the Corporation could not sustain the high level of finance and debt between Caxton and BPC and urged Caxton to take positive action either by way of a rights issue or sale of the company.

   b) I informed Caxton clearly and precisely that BPC was unable to bid for Caxton Holdings due to our own very substantial over-borrowed position. There could be no reason for Caxton to be in doubt on this issue.

   c) Entirely contrary to Caxton's comments of BPC's treatment of them, they expressed to me their pleasure and relief at BPC's new involvement in the company and the first time BPC was aware of contrary comments was indirectly after they left the company and through their evidence to the inspectors.

2)   The inspectors refer to the antedating of agreements. The BPC/ILSC agreements were dated within the financial year of the company upon the advice of the company's lawyers and with the knowledge of the company's auditors. These agreements evidenced transactions that had taken place in December 1967 including the transfer of shares and the payment of money. The inspectors in their report themselves concede that the auditors and the Inland Revenue would have

had no grounds for treating the accounts differently if the agreements had all been dated with the date on which they were executed. They also go to say that they are satisfied that there was no intention on anyone's part to defraud anyone and no one was defrauded. It could just have well have been said that they had no intention to deceive anyone and no one was deceived.

It is moreover difficult to see how I could have been more forthcoming with my evidence.

3) It is alleged that the first interim dividend was paid otherwise than out of profits. The body of the report refers to the evidence of the BPC directors on the ILSC board, including myself. I took considerable pains to see that the payment of the dividends came within the level of profits warranted by Pergamon Press. The inspectors state that contrary to the directors' belief at the time such profits would not have been available for distribution, but we have obtained leading council's opinion confirming that warranted profits are profits available for distribution. The second dividend was again approved by the BPC directors on the ILSC board similarly against the background of the warranty of profits referred to above and they gave evidence accordingly.

However, in the final accounts for 1968 for BPC, the second dividend was not credited to the profit and loss account but as a matter of prudence was carried to reserves. This decision was taken because the audited accounts of ILSC were not available at the time of the completion of the BPC accounts.

4) The annual report and accounts for BPC for the 52 weeks to the end of December 1968 are criticised for an inaccurate note relating to the treatment of dividends. This point was never put to the company. Notes 3, 9 and 11 to the accounts explain the matter precisely, clearly and correctly as should have been evident to the inspectors.

The whole report appears heavily influenced by the benefit of hindsight and whilst it is accepted that it was a mistake to become partners with Pergamon Press without obtaining any part of the executive management responsibility, I and other BPC directors maintain that they acted properly throughout the transaction.

BPC bought the remaining 10% of ILSC from Pergamon in 1972, by exercising its option in the 1970 agreement to purchase for cash at par (£200,000) the outstanding 10% of the ordinary share capital. ILSC was now a wholly owned subsidiary of BPC.

The Department of Trade and Industry published its final report of the inspector's findings on the affairs of Pergamon Press on November 20th. 1973, and on this same day BPC issued the following press statement:

"The British Printing Corporation has no involvement in any of the body of the final report, but is very pleased to note that, for the first time in the history of DTI reports, the inspectors have seen fit to correct certain important misconceptions in the first part of the report involving ILSC which refer to Mr. J.M.Pickard, deputy chairman of the British Printing Corporation.

This vindicates the contentions BPC has been making since the publication of the first report."

The final report contained a one-page chapter in which the inspectors admitted that their first report was more critical of Mr. Pickard than was justified in the light of their present knowledge.

At Purnells things were under control and, thankfully, profits were being generated, a fact that had not gone unnoticed by the main BPC board in 1971. At a meeting of directors of BPC, 140 from all companies attended, held in London, Sir Charles Hardie and Peter Robinson reviewed the corporation's progress and gave their opinions for further progress. In his review of the Purnell Group, Peter Robinson said:- "The Purnell Group has since 1966 shown most remarkable growth. It has in fact, been the backbone of Corporation profitability during the last three years. Again this year the group has been hit by the reduction in turnover from ILSC and by the loss of certain gravure mail order and pre-print work, but I regard this as a temporary setback. The returns are still excellent and I am sure the growth of former years will soon commence again.

This confidence in the Purnell Factory enabled a third heatset web offset press to be installed at Paulton the following year. This was a four unit M.A.N. web offset press with a web width of 52 inches (1,320mm.) and a cut off of 38.25 inches (972mm.). The maximum printing speed was 25,000 cylinder revolutions per hour. Peter Williams, the sales director of Purnell's said, "We had the magazine market very much in mind when we bought the M.A.N. press, but the versatility offered by the new press and its folder has already proved very useful

Frank Sullivan, Purnell's Web offset manager, receiving a certificate for outstanding technical achievement, in the Lithoprinter Offset Awards, from Miss Catherine Arthur, the Editor of Lithoprinter.

BPC announced that John Pollock was to leave BPC on March 31st. 1971 on terms mutually agreed. Since his direct responsibility for the Publishing Group ceased in late 1969, he had been working on the rationalisation of the worldwide activities of ILSC. Hugh Lavington, the former managing director of L.T.A.Robinson, joined Purnell gravure in the summer of 1971 as Gravure Works Manager.

The installation of web 3 in Purnell's at Paulton in 1972 in the space at the end of the old letterpress machine room: quite a distance from webs 1 and 2. In this picture, left to right: Just visible in the background are Joe Simmonds and E. Rogers, electricians working on the folder, C. Phillips, printers assistant on the steps, R. Rogers, assistant, and printer J. Bamford on the floor.

The original farmhouse of Manor Farm Paulton had been used by Purnells as an office since the early 1930's and became the Registered Office, in 1935, of Purnell & Sons Ltd. Approximately 400 years old, its timbers were now riddled with woodworm and suffering from dry rot, it was said that they had previously seen service as ships' timbers; the building had to be replaced. In 1971 a new office building was constructed, faced in local stone in keeping with the original farmhouse. The new office offered twice the floor space than that which was available before. The garden flanking the approach to the reception area with its beautiful shrubs and plants became a car park.

The original Manor Farmhouse, used as offices, before its demolition in 1971.

A less happy event of 1972 was that on February 21st., Barrow Paper Mills were to close with a loss of employment for some 200 men and 70 women. The mill had been founded in the 1880's, Wilfred Harvey had invested in this company in 1955, when paper supplies were unreliable, and took complete control in December 1961 when Purnells acquired the remaining capital of the British Coated Board and Paper Company, his younger son Geoffrey was managing director of this mill up to the time of his premature death.

The BPC announcement said: "The closure has come after three years of substantial losses and in spite of strenuous efforts to carry on, at a time when every paper mill making woodfree grades is finding survival difficult. The Corporation has at last had to concede, however, that the Barrow paper mill is at a permanent disadvantage, especially against foreign competition, and there is no alternative to closure.

Purnells obtained a useful contract in 1973, from Headway Publications, to print British Airways in- flight magazine "Highlife", issue No.1 came out in April 1973. This magazine was printed on Web 3 for a few years. William Davies, an ex-editor of Punch magazine, edited Highlife and often visited the Paulton factory; later in1975 he was asked to edit the Barclay's Bank magazine "Advantage" which Purnells also printed. Another magazine that helped Web 3 to keep busy, was the Diners Club magazine "Signature", this had a run of 170,000 and printed every two months.

Following the death of Peter Lavington on the 20th.December 1974, some top managerial changes were made at Paulton. Eric Harvey was appointed Chairman of Purnells, Peter Robinson, the former chairman still remaining on the Purnell board. W. J. Harvey (Bill) was appointed sole managing director of Purnell
In October 1975 Sir Charles Hardie declared that he was to retire after the next AGM in May 1976, and that Peter Robinson would succeed him as executive chairman. Sir Charles said that he would reach 65 years of age this year and he must reduce his business commitments.

Sam Wright, the Purnell personnel director, who succeeded Arthur Cornish, who had died in 1973, left the corporation in 1977 to take up the position of Director of the Industrial Relations Training Centre at Ashridge Management Centre in Hertfordshire. Michael McBennet was appointed personnel director of Purnell. Michael was personnel manager of Jarrolds in Norwich from 1965 and previously he had spent five years with the London Fire Brigade and eleven years with the Ford Motor Company.

In 1977 Lord Kings Norton left the BPC board and so did Terence Kenny. Roy Hodgson joined the board of BPC as personnel director, Roy had been in print most of his life, he was apprenticed in 1946 and became a NGA regional officer in 1966, he joined the Print House staff in 1972.

Back at Paulton, Eddie Hounsell the sales executive that looked after the Deans account for Purnell retired after 42 years with the company. Eddie was a very popular man at Purnells, he joined Purnell in 1934 and worked closely with Wilfred Harvey in building up the Woolworth account, it eventually reached £1,000,000 annually, in servicing 1,100 Woolworth stores with only two assistants, but then computers came in and he moved to the Deans account. In 1936 he took over the captaincy of Purnell's cricket club from Wilfred Harvey and also became the fixtures secretary and has had the job ever since! Eddie will never forget that Wilfred Harvey had two bell pushes on his desk; one was for the chief accountant and the other was for him.

A new publishing company was created in 1972-called Phoebus and was installed in Poland Street, London, to publish part-works for BPC. The managing director was Fred Newman, the commercial director Gerd Seeber, managing editor John Paton, and the production manager was Don Mason. "The History of the 20th.Century" was re-launched in February 1973 with an initial run of 300,000 on the webs at Purnells. BPC's first short-term part-work "Get Slim and Stay Slim" followed in March, printed by Pettys. Considerable success was met with the one-shot magazines, "War Planes", "Tank Story", "First War Planes", "Weapons of War" and "War Ships and Submarines" all in 1973, the latter titles being printed at Waterlows.

Purnell Books Publishers removed themselves from Poland Street and relocated at Maidenhead and according to Charles Harvey, the general manager of Purnell Books, they had no regrets about leaving, as the offices they were moving to were those recently vacated by a prestigious American computer bureau and the standard of fixtures and fittings were somewhat higher than those usually seen in BPC. Maidenhead was also convenient for access to Paulton and London.

Purnell Books had a record year in 1973. Mail-order and cash-and - carry business doubled and the Disney sales went up by 60%. All of this meant more work for the factory at Paulton and the Service Centre.

Mr. Paterson, the former chairman of Purnells, and who was managing director of H.G.Bentley, retired and Arnold Bentley succeeded him as chairman of H.G.Bentley in 1975.

February 1975 the Nickeloid factory in Union Street, London, SE1 closed down (not the Waterloo Road factory).

A Roland six colour, size 7 (1600x 1,100mm.) sheet fed offset being installed in the Litho Pressroom at Paulton. Brian Bushell, the press overseer and Mr. Jones, the press minder are looking at a lot of Printing press.

Bill Harvey, Purnell's deputy chairman, who had been suffering from a long illness died on the 23rd.February 1979 at the age of 56, he left a widow and three sons. Bill joined Purnells in 1947 and during the 32 years he spent at Purnells as manager and director, he got to know everyone in all the departments and he also took a keen interest in the sports and social activities of the company.

Hazell Watson & Viney Ltd. at Aylesbury, Buckinghamshire had printed the Reader's Digest magazine since 1951 on a Goss letterpress rotary machine. Hazells also typeset and bound the magazine in house. In 1979 it was decided to print the magazine by gravure at Purnells; the Goss machine at Hazells was by now outdated and slow and was getting expensive to maintain. Hazells retained the typesetting and the binding, the latter meant transporting the printed sections a 100 miles each month by road. Hazells used Sheridan perfect binding machines, employing the two-shot adhesive system, that used a first application of cold P.V.A. adhesive that was dried with a radiant gas heater before the hotmelt, a non-aqueous adhesive, was applied at speeds of up to 6,000 clamps per hour. The magazines were bound two-up, with a coming and going imposition. The bound result was a very strong, durable, yet flexible spine; hence the customers desire to continue the binding operation at Aylesbury for the time being.

As the decade drew to a close the printing capacity at Paulton was very large. There were 43 units of gravure available and this was to be shortly increased to 53 units, there were five Roland 4 colour presses and one 6-colour press, three single colour-perfecting presses, two ATF web offset presses and one MAN web offset press

The binding department now had three Martini perfect binding machines as well as a very large cased binding section, offering most styles of binding. Folding and wire stitching had also kept up to date; some of the knife folding machines had been replaced with MBO buckle folding machines, which doubled the output. The Sheridan Pacesetter inserters and stitchers handled the wire-stitched work with ease.

The company obtained some very useful print and bind orders from the Milk Marketing Board, which kept Web 3 busy and the cased bindery, the titles were "The Dairy Book of Home Cookery" and "Home Management". The company was even treated to some glamour from visits from the Dairy Queens during the 1970's.

Donald McIntosh, the Managing Director of Purnell Main Division, presenting the current, reigning Dairy Queen for 1979/80 with a gift during her visit to Paulton, accompanied by John Steer, manager of R. Somerville, Paper Mill, Somerset.

The BPC profit record of the 1970's: -

Year	Sales, 000	Trading Profit, (Loss) 000	Interest Paid	Profit (Loss) before Tax	Tax	Profit (Loss) After Tax
1970	76,349	(273)	(2,06)	(2,679)	1,364	(1,315)
1971	75,224	3,617	(2,137)	1,480	(400)	1,080
1972	78,817	5,579,	(1,763)	4,060	(1,205)	2,855
1973	89,734	6,922	(1,706)	5,168	(1,042)	4,126
1974	112,735	8,047	(2,657)	4,524	(1,371)	3,153
1975	127,518	7,037	(3,116)	3,122	(1,611)	1,511
1976	143,594	8,004	(3,440)	4,756	(2,234)	2,522
1977	154,863	9,433	(3,494)	5,788	(1,918)	3,870
1978	174,084	11,132	(3,715)	7,125	(2,364)	4,761

The Purnell publishing interests within BPC underwent some changes in the 1970's. As previously stated, following the departure of Richard Holme and Peter Galliner early in the decade, John Pollock left the corporation, on terms mutually agreed, on March 31st. 1971. Since John Pollock's direct responsibility for the Publishing Group ceased in 1969, he had been working on the rationalisation of the worldwide activities of ILSC. Richard Masterman became the new Managing Director of ILSC.

Eric Harvey was appointed a BPC director on April 30th. 1971, and was made responsible for the Purnell Group of companies, he resigned his Publishing Group Directorship.

Eric Harvey and Michael Bell of Walt Disney Productions (U.K.) Ltd signed up the Walt Disney contract in 1971, for three years. Charles Harvey, publisher of Bancroft Books, said that in the last three years over six million Disney books have been sold by Purnells

Publishing now comprised:
BPC Publishing Ltd.	at Poland Street
Partworks	Poland Street
Macdonald & Co.	Poland Street
Purnell Book Services	Poland Street
Promotion Services	Paulton House

The sale of the Haymarket Press back to Michael Hesseltine was completed on the 7th. April 1971.

In November 1971 BPC also got out of the greeting card business by selling Raphael Tuck & Sons, W. Barton (Publishers), and British Greeting Cards to Fine Art Developments for a consideration of approximately £650,000. Also to go were the toys and games businesses of Philmar Ltd. and Ariel Ltd. to Boxes Ltd.

Futura paperback publishers was formed in 1973, the Managing Director was Anthony Cheatham and the first title of the newly formed company, "The Pallisers", was published on 18th. April 1974.

Although Purnells were not paperback-book printers and binders, they ended up storing hundreds of thousands of these paperbacks in the late

1980's when the original litho-press room and pre-press areas were racked out to accommodate them.

CHAPTER TWELVE

THE 1980'S

The board of Purnell & Sons Ltd., at the beginning of the 1980's, was as follows, Chairman O. P. Hassell, Joint Managing Directors P. A. Lavington and Donald McIntosh, Directors Peter Robinson, D. B. Bailey F.C.A., P. O.Williams, A. M. Alfred, K. R. Brown, M. F. McBennet and C. Harvey.

The poor financial performance of BPC during the last year of the 1970's had a disastrous effect on the share value of the company.
On July 18th.1980 Robert Maxwell, the proprietor of Pergamon Press, staged a dawn raid on BPC through broker Grieveson Grant and acquired 29.5% of BPC's capital for £2.9 million in a space of 12 minutes. The price per share paid was 25p.

Robert Maxwell had a well - publicised meeting with Peter Robinson and the former Chairman of BPC, Sir Charles Hardie, where discussions took place on what work Pergamon could possibly place with BPC and what possible boardroom representation could Pergamon have with BPC. The meetings were to be continued, but the next meeting happened to be one held at the Office of Fair Trading.

This was not the first time that BPC had become involved with Robert Maxwell, it will be recalled that the joint venture on International Learning Systems Corporation, in the 1970's had caused some embarrassment and difficulties for the company. But with the 1979 profit only £398,000 after tax and the 1980 profit prediction zero, or even a loss, on sales of £200,000,000 as predicted at August 1980, there was little the BPC directors could do to stop the downward slide in BPC's share value. Attempts to decrease interest charges were made by selling some assets such as Jane's Publishing Company to Thomson Books for £3,150,000 on the 7th. August 1980.

Jane's Publishing was bought by Wilfred Harvey, as part of Sampson Low Marston & Co. in 1941, when Percy White, who was ill, asked Wilfred Harvey to buy his shares in the company; this was a controlling interest. Frederick T Jane had started the company in 1898 and over the years it has become well known for publishing such well known titles as, Jane's Fighting Ships, Jane's All the World's Aircraft and The World's Railways. A story is told that during the Second World War, the British Naval Intelligence had no information on the specification of the German E-Boats until someone popped out and bought a copy of Jane's Fighting Ships.

Mr. Maxwell also bid for Jane's, on behalf of Pergamon, offering a higher price and offered an option to sell it back to BPC if they thought they needed it back, but it was ignored.

At Paulton, the Gravure Division had a problem in mid 1980, the Observer newspaper was under threat of closure due to industrial relation problems at the printers and this threatened the Observer Magazine printed at Paulton. Michael McBenett put up the following notice on the 17th. July: -

WORKS NOTICE

You will know of the problems facing the Observer and the possibility of that newspaper closing down, resulting in a loss to us of the magazine.
We have been repeatedly asked for a Press Statement and at midday today we released the following text:

> 'The management and employees of Purnell & Sons Limited are deeply concerned over the problems confronting the

Observer newspaper and hope that a speedy solution will be found.

The issues involved are outside the control of Purnell, which has been printing the Observer Colour Magazine from its inception.

Should the Observer newspaper close – and with it the Colour Magazine – it will not only represent a major loss to the newspaper world but will undoubtedly cause hardship among the employees at Paulton, many of whom would lose their jobs.

Purnell produces a wide variety of periodicals, catalogues and books and loss of the Observer Magazine would come at a time of a general reduction in trading activity'

We have no more news than that which is already written up in this mornings newspapers, but we do promise,that as soon as any firm developments arise, whether it be good news or bad, we will inform you as soon as we can.

M. F. McBennett

On the 21st.July 1980, Mr. O. P. Hassell, the chairman of Purnells, put up the following Works Notice:-

WORKS NOTICE

Mr. Peter Williams has resigned to take up another appointment and he is now absent on leave for the duration of his notice period, which expires by mutual agreement on 30th.September.
I take this opportunity to thank Peter for his many years of service to Purnell, which have been of great value to us all, to

record the regret of all his colleagues and friends in the company, and to give him, his wife and family the best of good wishes for the future.

O.P. Hassell
Chairman

An update notice on the Observer Colour Magazine situation was put up on the 30th July 1980:-

WORKS NOTICE

THE OBSERVER

You will know that the proposed agreement drawn up during discussions held with A.C.A.S. and between N.G.A. and the Observer management has been rejected by the Observer Machine Room Chapel. In a further attempt to solve the issue the Observer management accepted the request made by N.G.A. at the weekend for individual notices of dismissal not to be issued pending the intervention of the T.U.C. and its General Secretary, Mr. Murray.

Today, however, with no apparent prospect of a solution in sight, the Observer has issued the following statement to the Press Association:-

The National Graphical Association advised the Observer on Monday that the management's offer which the Association recommended to the Machine Managers' Chapel was rejected by some 26 members of the Chapel on Saturday. This offer followed the intervention of A.C.A.S. last week.

The offer of pay, staffing and holidays which the Company made after many months of negotiations was generous. The rate of pay for a single Saturday night shift, which was rejected, is close to the national average earnings for a full week's work. Through relief working none of the men concerned works for the full shift.

The Company, in accordance with decisions communicated some time ago to the General Secretaries of all the trades unions with members at the Observer, is giving notice to all its staff, amounting to over 1,000 people whose employment will end in October.

The Company deeply regrets the necessity for this course of action.

We have been instructed by the Observer to run down paper stocks of the Magazine and they have informed us that the issue dated 19th.October 1980 will be the last.

The closure of the Observer will be bad news for us coinciding, as it will with an already deteriorating trading position in both Gravure and Main. It is clear that the Directors will have to think hard about the future. They will be in discussions with managers and representatives when the position at the Observer becomes more clear.

M.F. McBennett

The amount of money being disputed at the end of the Observer Newspaper negotiations appeared small. Agreement had already been achieved on a rate of £93.63 for a 48-page paper. The union reduced its £108.03 claim for a 64-page paper, but wanted the extra payment of £6.50, offered by management to be paid for a 56-page paper.

Following Peter Williams' departure, the board of the gravure division needed restructuring. On the 21st. November 1980 the following notice appeared:-

WORKS NOTICE

The following changes to the composition of the board of Purnell & Sons Ltd. will take effect as from Monday, 29th. December 1980.

Gravure Division and Bristol Photo Engraving Ltd.
Mr. Michael McBennett will assume responsibility for this Division and is appointed a director of Bristol Photo Engraving Ltd.

Personnel Management and Industrial Relations

Mr.Keith Morris has been appointed to the board of Purnell & Sons Ltd. Mr. Morris worked for many years with Bradbury Wilkinson Ltd. and is currently Group Personnel Director of the Williams Lea Group.

O. P. Hassell
Chairman

Things were not improving financially at BPC, the sterling exchange rate was eroding margins and foreign competition was getting intense, particularly with colour book printing and mail-order catalogue printing. Purnell was heavily into both of these markets.

The board of BPC had resisted having Mr. Maxwell joining them throughout 1980, although he owned 29.5% of the equity of the company. BPC was desperate for a substantial capital injection but the institutions had had enough of BPC. The BPC directors had attempted to refer Mr. Maxwell's holding in BPC to the Monopolies Commission by an approach to the Office of Fair Trading, in an attempt to stop Mr. Maxwell taking control of BPC. However, Mr. John Nott, the Trade Secretary, decided that this was not necessary, therefore leaving Mr. Maxwell in a position to bid for the rest of the shares. It was reported in the press that Mr. Maxwell was upset at the tactics used by the BPC directors during the OFT hearings, which he regarded as a personal attack upon him.

Monty Alfred, one of BPC's directors spoke to an old colleague from his Courtauld days, Lord Kearton and suggested he cast his eye over some projections on the BPC trading position. Lord Kearton, a director of the merchant bank Hill Samuel and former chairman of Courtauld was appalled by what he saw and made overtures to the Bank of England and the Government, through his contacts in these areas, on behalf of BPC. The response was that every one thought BPC too far gone at this stage and no help was forthcoming. BPC's interim statement showed that the company had lost £6.5 million in the first half of 1981, on sales approaching £100 million.

Lord Kearton finally persuaded the BPC board that any help could only come from private enterprise and he outlined his views to Robert Maxwell whose Pergamon Press had £10,000,000 available and he owned 29.5% of BPC anyway. The directors of BPC finally invited Robert Maxwell to join the board. There was a fear that when Mr. Maxwell saw the extent of the difficulty that BPC was in, he would back off, but he didn't and a rescue package was prepared to put before the BPC's shareholders. Pergamon Press would now hold almost 77% of BPC's equity; Robert Maxwell would be the Chief Executive and Lord Kearton, the new non-executive chairman from February 1981.

The rescue plan contained the aims of the corporation based on Mr. Maxwell's study tour of 40 of BPC's 42 printing centres. The main objectives were to reduce the workforce of about 10,500 by 2,700, this included management, stop paying the large pay increases of recent times although the national pay award of £7.50 would be honoured. Productivity also must be a priority for management. Mr. Maxwell also saw the leaders of the print unions and got their endorsement for his rescue plan. The National Westminster Bank also was willing to put in extra funds by increasing its overdraft limit from £32.5million to £41.5 million and was offering a concessionary rate of 5% annually on £10 million of any continuing overdraft for this year and next. This being subject to the shareholders agreement.

The share value of BPC had sunk to an all time low of 15p per share when Robert Maxwell increased Pergamon's holding to 77% in BPC. This represented a loss of £1.4 million on his original investment in BPC when he made his dawn- raid in July 1980.

On the 24th.February 1981 the following notice was posted in Purnells:-

COMPANY NOTICE

On his visit to Paulton today Mr. Robert Maxwell, Chief Executive of BPC Limited said this was the first BPC plant he had visited where he had been able to make a formal commitment. He said:

"I have come to deliver the decision that Paulton will stay open providing that we can get agreement with trade unions and staff for reductions in operating costs and staffing levels which will enable the Company to break-even in 1981. I have had very satisfactory discussions with the print unions concerned – with Mr. Joe Wade of the N.G.A., Mr. Owen O'Brien of NATSOPA, Mr. Bill Keys of SOGAT and Mr John Jackson of SLADE, and have been assured of their wholehearted co-operation to assist me in the restructuring of BPC so as to return it to its former profitability and viability. Purnell's management under Mr.Peter Hassell, the Chairman, will be presented to the chapels for consultation, a document detailing the kind of savings that the workforce will be asked to contribute to, including changes in working practices that will make Purnell & Sons Limited competitive with any other company in the UK or Europe for gravure printing and book production etc."

The management will start the consultations by the end of this week.

O.P. HASSELL

24 .2 .81

All the BPC companies were presenting their individual plans to Robert Maxwell in the ensuing weeks and Purnells presented theirs in mid March 1981 at London.

The cut back at Purnell was severe, most of the redundancies fell on Purnell Main Division and Western Ink Limited. A Works Notice was posted on the 18th.March 1981:

WORKS NOTICE

THE FOLLOWING PRESS RELEASE WAS MADE AT NOON TODAY 18th.MARCH, 1981.

Mr. Peter Hassell, Chairman of Purnell & Sons Limited, regrets to announce the decision reached by the Board of BPC Limited, its parent company, to drastically reduce its operations in book production and distribution due to the impact of the recession and the strength of overseas competition.

Approximately 800 jobs will be lost by the end of June. A specialised book printing and binding unit will continue in the future on the premises employing 180 people.
There will be no redundancies in Purnell Gravure Printing Division, but agreements have been reached in principle with Union Representatives, which incorporate changes in working practices designed to secure economies.

Mr.Maxwell, Deputy Chairman and Chief Executive of BPC Limited is expected to meet General Secretaries of the Print Unions later this week to endorse agreements for the restructuring of all BPC subsidiaries including Purnell.

Mr. Maxwell has approved a £1 million investment programme for Purnell Book production activities and further heavy investment in Gravure is expected later.

Western Ink Limited, also owned by BPC will be making 17 redundancies in response to reduced demand from Purnell and other sister companies.

On the 8th. June 1981 the following notice about the restructuring of Purnell's businesses at Paulton was posted: -

WORKS NOTICE

Effective from the 1st.July 1981, the present business of the Company will be split into three separate management units. For the remainder of 1981 these units will remain a part of Purnell & Sons Ltd., but as from 1st. January 1982 , separate companies will be formed to take over the Book Printing, Publishing, and Service Centre – Data Processing businesses.

 The names of these three companies operating on the Paulton site will be: -

Purnell & Sons Limited – this will continue the business currently known as Purnell Gravure.

Chairman	- Robert Maxwell
Managing Director	- P.A. Lavington
Works Director	- M.F. McBennett
Personnel Director	- K. Morris
Director	- J.W. Hooke
Director	- R. Hodgson
Director	- D.C. Moore

Purnell & Sons (Book Production) Limited -this is the company name for the new book production unit.

Chairman	- M. Pegge
Managing Director	- K.R. Brown

Non-executive Director - Robert Maxwell
Non-executive Director - D. McIntosh

Purnell Publishers Limited – the business of Purnell Books and the combined Service Centre and Data Processing departments will be carried out under this company name.

Chairman   - Robert Maxwell
Managing Director   - D.B. Bailey
Non-executive Director - D. McIntosh

Other appointments relating to the new companies will be announced in due course.

P.A. Lavington

The major upheaval in the new set up was the establishing of the new book production unit, which meant that the pre-press, sheet fed litho, and bindery departments had to be physically relocated in a smaller, more economical to run, area in the centre of the Paulton site. All this without a too damaging loss of production time as customers still wanted their books on time.

The new management team of Purnell & Sons (Book Production) Ltd. was as follows: -

Chairman   - Michael Pegge
Managing Director   - Keith Brown
Works Director   - Terry Goodman
Sales and Commercial Director - David Adnett
Personnel Director   - John Raine
Finance Director   - Eddie Parker

The new company had no composing department now and all type matter arrived as film supplied, mainly by the customers, although a special section was created to buy in typesetting and colour separations, as a customer service; the Gravure Division's Linotron 505 system, used for typesetting the Observer Magazine was also available to the book company.

The envelope department was retained, this was the only section kept by Purnells from the Runprint sale in 1967. Greeting card envelopes and commercial envelopes were the speciality with an annual capacity of some 150 million envelopes.

Tony Wilmot managed the pre-press department and the relocation gave the opportunity to ensure that the new department was as modern, clean and efficient as any other plate producing concern.
A new Misomex Master imposition machine was bought to augment the existing Misomex step and repeat machine.

The litho pressroom had two shift managers, Tony Jones and Brian Bushell. The presses retained were:-
> Roland Ultra VII 6 Colour
> Roland Ultra VII 4 Colour
> Crabtree SP 65 Perfector
> Koenig and Bauer Rapida 4 Colour 720x520mm.
> MAN Ultraman 5 colour 1600 x 1100mm.

The latter was a new press, specified and bought by the new company with co-edition bookwork very much in mind. Purnells had become experts over the years in running two black plates when printing four colour books in several languages; the text plates, separate from the colour half-tones, could quickly be changed without disturbing the colour register.
There were no web offset presses in the new company.
Both the pressroom and the plate making room were air-conditioned and the factory was now, more or less, on one level rather than several levels of considerable height differences.

The bindery was managed by Ron Laidler and incorporated the folding and wire stitching sections. The cased bindery had two Kolbus lines, a EMP 40 Line and a EMP 70 Line for flat backed books. Case making was done on two Dexter machines, one Kolbus DA 36, and one Sheridan end feed casemaker. The sewing department had eight Brehmer 385 machines, four Smyth 18 machines and Singer sewing available. The wire stitching was done on a Sheridan 8 station inserter with a 5 knives trimmer.

The management team for Purnell & Sons were all experienced in the printing trade in general and some in book production in particular.

Keith Brown, Managing Director, came to Purnells in 1977, as Works Director, from W.S.Cowell in East Anglia, where he was Works Director. Keith was a Justice of the Peace and sat on the Bath Bench.

Terry Goodman, Works Director, came to Purnells in 1976 from Western Book Company where he was joint Managing Director and before that General Manager of BPC's, Hazell Watson & Viney's book plant in Wales

David Adnett, Sales and Commercial Director, a Purnell man trained by Donald McIntosh in costing and estimating, with a good sales knowledge of the Children's book business.

John Raine, Personnel Director, another Purnell man who had been in the personnel department and was experienced in all aspects of the job, including Industrial Relations and Health and Safety matters.

Eddie Parker, Finance Director, had been with Purnell for many years assisting the Company Secretary and had been responsible for the Purnell Group Companies.

One of the Corporations largest contracts, that was being negotiated at the same time that Mr. Maxwell made his dawn raid on BPC, was the TV Times magazine, printed hitherto at Eric Bemrose Ltd
Independent Television Publications wanted to improve the schedule and increase the pagination to 112 pages; this meant investment of about £20 million in new equipment and Bemrose could not see their way clear to manage this. The contract was worth £120 million, (£18 million a year) and was due to commence in August 1981.

BPC companies were involved in this production, but Purnell was not, for example Waterlows would do the 13 regions typesetting, Sun would do the gravure printing and needed two, 13 unit, gravure presses, costing £11 million, M1 Studios, Chromoworks, Pettys, Carlisle Web Offset, these all required a total of another £7 million
to operate the contract. It could be seen that a lot of BPC companies were not going to get the investment that they needed and had to join the long queue. Purnells were lucky; they got their promised amount.

Mr. Maxwell himself notified more management changes on the 7th May 1982, at Purnell Gravure: -

PURNELL & SONS LTD.

MANAGEMENT CHANGES AND APPOINTMENTS

The following changes will take immediate effect: -

FINANCE AND COMMERCIAL

Mr.E.I. WOOD is redesignated FINANCIAL & COMMERCIAL DIRECTOR.
Mr. R. CAVILL is appointed CHIEF ACCOUNTANT responsible to Mr. Wood.
Mr. J. RICHARDSON, COMMERCIAL MANAGER will now be responsible to Mr. Wood.

THE 1980'S

TECHNICAL SALES

Mr. B. WOODMAN is appointed TECHNICAL SALES MANAGER responsible to Mr. Morris, Managing Director. Mr. WOODMAN will be particularly accountable for ensuring that customers' standards of quality are met and also for customer liaison in general. Mr. K. SEYMOUR and Mr. K. HAND are appointed ACCOUNT EXECUTIVES responsible to Mr. WOODMAN.

BRISTOL PHOTO ENGRAVING

Mr. P. MARSHALL is appointed B. P. E. PROCESS MANAGER responsible to the Managing Director not only for providing cylinders at the right quality and price but also for pursuing the introduction of new techniques and technology while understanding the human factors attending these. Mr. R. BENNET is appointed QUALITY CONTROL MANAGER, B.P.E., responsible to MR. Marshall. Mr. Bennett's task will be to improve quality throughout B.P.E., and to obtain consistency in results. He will liase with Mr. Woodman regarding customer's requirements.

TECHNICAL PROJECTS

Mr. D. YENDOLE is appointed PROJECTS MANAGER responsible to the Managing Director. Mr. Yendole will be involved in studies designed to improve costs and efficiency. He will also continue the liaison with Mr. C. Rowe and Mr. A. Grainger, B.P.E. and Gravure Technical Managers to ensure a consistent thrust in our technical development.

ENGINEERING SERVICES

Mr. C.N. LUNT, Engineering Services Manager will now be responsible to the Managing Director. Mr. M.F. HARVEY, formerly Chief Engineer, Purnell Main, and Mr. D. CORNISH, Chief Engineer,

Purnell Gravure, will now be responsible to Mr. Lunt. Mr. Harvey continues to be involved in the re-organisation of parts of the site outside the Gravure Division and B.P.E. Because of this the description of the duties Mr. Harvey and Mr. Cornish will eventually be asked to perform will be announced later in the year.

PERSONNEL & RELATED SERVICES

Mr. G. MOLLARD is appointed PERSONNEL MANAGER responsible to the Deputy Managing Director, Mr. M.F. McBennett. Mr.Mollard will initially be involved in redeveloping the ancillary services such as Safety, Medical, Fire and Security, Catering and the Pensions Consultative aspects. He will eventually play a part in all aspects of personnel work including industrial relations. In addition Mr. Mollard will link with Mr. Wood on Pensions Administration work.

ROBERT MAXWELL
CHAIRMAN

7.5.82

Things were not going too well in the Gravure Division during 1982 from a profitability viewpoint. There were three gravure factories in BPCC, Sun, Odhams and Purnell, it was obvious to some that one would have to go, as orders were diminishing due to European competition and some of the presses were overdue for renewal.
The managers and union representatives received this statement, from the company, on the 13th. July 1982:-

COMPANY VIABILITY

PHASE 1

As you all know, Purnell Gravure is trading at a heavy loss this year. That is still the position and very accurate estimates are that our loss will be just under a million pounds, in fact, £910,000.

During the course of many meetings we have explored many ways in which the workforce and the management can effect economies and savings which will help Purnell to recover from this heavy loss making position and satisfy Robert Maxwell and the BPCC board that the assurance of no redundancy during 1982 can be continued.

The most optimistic measure we can put on the proposals the chapels are prepared to agree is of the order of £50,000 per annum. I know you are still in the process of discussing as chapels what further savings can be made but now I have reached the position where I must in a very short time give BPCC the Purnell Strategy for 1983. I cannot do that based on existing operations unless I have a definite indication of the savings we will make this year.

Robert Maxwell put it squarely to us that it is in our hands as to how we underwrite Purnell for 1983 and beyond. The Purnell board has decided that we are prepared to fight very hard with Robert Maxwell for a Business Plan that has the following features:-

1. That we must have quantified and precisely definite savings from all chapels which amount to cost reductions in a full year of at least £500.000.

2. We do want to appear to be imposing our solution because any business plan will fail if we do not work together to make it succeed. For this reason we can see a number of ways of achieving the £500,000 cost savings and I am putting them to you today as options for the chapels to consider but with the definite requirement that some, if not all, of them must be agreed between us in order to achieve the £500,000 cost saving target. The measures which will help us to achieve this target are:-

A. As a company we wish to make a definite requirement of a change in the holiday pay calculations with effect from 1st. October 1982 which will be based on the average of the previous ten weeks earnings. This will give us a saving in a full year of £250,000.

B.   The approach to the other £250,000 savings can be achieved in a number of different ways and the chapels might want to consider cover during absences for holidays/sickness, temporary staffing reductions, reduction in overtime premiums, or any other suggestions you might have.

This plan is now deadlined and requires an urgent response from you so that we can prepare our 1983 Strategy and Budgets, which we have to have completed by end July this year. If the chapels have any difficulty in their co-operation then I suggest that you should immediately seek the help of National Officers of your unions so that talks can proceed speedily. The alternative is that Management will have to put in a Business Plan for 1983 which will not be what we would like, nor what the workforce would like but which commercial and market realities will demand.

Our proposal is that whatever measures we agree to bring through the £500,000 savings, should operate for 12 months and be subject to review in a year's time so that both you and we will have the chance to judge Purnell's position in the then prevailing market.

PHASE II

After we have established the £500,000 savings we should enter into immediate talks relating to new investment and changes in working practices which will be required as a result of the new equipment and the need to change working patterns and staffing levels.

We cannot proceed to order equipment until we have agreement the new working arrangements. We need this during September this year.

PHASE III

If we are successful in agreeing to Phases 1 and 2 then I propose a final stage which you may regard as revolutionary but is an earnest intention to consult on all matters concerning the Company's future.
It is that with any major contract or jobbing enquiry we will discuss with the chapel officers what arrangements you are prepared to make to underwrite prices we can quote which will give us a competitive edge.

We can go into this more fully at the time but the essence of this is that the business is ours jointly and although management's job is to secure sales, how we produce and make our sales more efficient is as much in your hands as in the managements. There must be ways that we can together influence how we can convince customers to put their work with us.

This becomes even more important as BPCC has publicly declared its intention to introduce from the end of the year a profit sharing scheme. Bonuses will be paid on company performance and we therefore have a vested interest in a quick return to profitability.

K. MORRIS

Managing Director

13.7.82

It was found necessary to post another statement, addressed to all who work at Purnell & Sons Ltd., on the 2nd. August 1982:-

Dear Colleague,

<u>On the need to take immediate steps to reduce heavy losses and to avoid substantial reductions in employment.</u>

You will know that:

    i.   Purnells will lose some £900, 000 to £1,000,000 this year or £40 per week for every person employed in the company.

    ii.   Our company is suffering a severe shortage of work because of acute UK and continental gravure competition coupled with severe domestic web offset competition.

    iii.   The economy is at its worst since the 1930's, and not improving.

    iv.   There have been many continuing discussions with the representatives of all chapels over the past several weeks on these serious problems.

    v.   The company must, with everybody's help and co-operation take immediate measures to eliminate this unsupportable deficit.

In April Mr. Maxwell, while making all of us aware of the company's projected loss, took the unusual yet very fair decision to allow a pay award at Purnells without any strings attached. He simply stated the facts of the situation and pointed out that ' if we over priced ourselves in the marketplace the customer would walk away and we would have no jobs left'. We were all adult people and he left it to all of us to sort out our own survival. Given an indication of this he promised the investment we so sorely need. He stated 'that if management and the work force took the necessary measures to eliminate or substantially reduce the losses, he would be prepared to make substantial additional investment in equipment and sales efforts to ensure our survival and prosperity'.

Since that time, management and chapel officers have been engaged in one discussion after another. There may at one time have been some disbelief at what management were saying and this could still be the case with some people notwithstanding the fact that we have supplied all the information asked for. The document attached, entitled 'COMPANY VIABILITY' gives the stark facts and measures submitted by management to the trade union side for their consideration and support. We have received a lot of sympathy for the company's point of view, and a modest suggestion for cost reductions, such as a reduction in holiday pay entitlement and alteration to the number of people that may be away at any one time.

Unfortunately, these welcome suggestions totalled no more than approximately £10,000 in 1982 and £70,000 in 1983. You will all readily see in the light of the above facts that this is quite insufficient to save the company from closure or very heavy redundancies.

Whilst I accept that in normal times it is not the job of chapel officers to agree to recommend reductions in benefits, these are not normal times! This is a grave emergency and unpalatable action must be taken in the interests of ensuring the survival of Purnell's.

The position is such that if we do not reduce our costs now, we will not be able to hold even some of our major contracts nor gain the jobbing sales we so desperately need.

In view of the very grave economic situation the Board of Directors of Purnell's have no alternative but to announce the following economy measures:

1. To reduce the number of directors from nine to five. The directors retiring are, in alphabetical order:
   Mr. Hodgson
   Mr. Hooke

Mr. McIntosh
Mr. Moore
· The remaining directors will take a cut of 5% in their salary with immediate effect.

2. Managers who have been putting in overtime and who by old established practice were in receipt of an annual Christmas bonus, amounting in total to £15,000 per annum, have agreed to forego it.

3. Directors, mangers and office staff will reduce their holiday entitlement from five weeks to four weeks.

4. To give three months notice to all employees that with effect from the 1st. November, holiday pay will be based on the average earnings of the previous 10 weeks and not at the inflated rate, which was negotiated at a time when Purnells was full of work and highly profitable.

These immediate steps that we have taken will only partially contribute towards reducing our unacceptable losses. Other measures must be considered and implemented as soon as possible. Some of the measures and suggestions are in the Company Viability document a copy of which is attached. It goes without saying that the chapels and employees may have other ideas and concrete suggestions which may help us. Management does not claim a monopoly of ideas and measures that should be taken.
I know that I can rely on your understanding and positive co-operation to see Purnells through this very difficult and trying period, which if we survive and get through can be turned greatly to our medium and long-term advantage.

Yours sincerely,

Keith Morris
Managing Director

Purnell's losses continued through 1983 and Robert Maxwell's patience was getting a little strained, as he could not perceive any movement towards cost savings. A letter was sent out to the gravure staff on 16th. March 1984, by P.A. Lavington, Chief Executive of Purnell:-

Dear Employee,

I wrote to you on 2nd March to tell you that it was essential to reach agreement by the 15th March, with implementation by end of March; if Purnells is to avoid closure and achieve modernisation, through the investment of £17.2 million, necessary for us to hold and obtain work at competitive prices from customers at home and abroad.

The loss of work, constant delays in meeting customer requirements and the refusal to implement new developments, processes and techniques have restricted the company's ability to obtain work in an extremely competitive market place. Consequently, over the past three years Purnell's trading position has deteriorated rapidly and since January 1982 the Company's losses have amounted to £1,971,000. In 1983 the losses were equivalent to a subsidy of £2,573 per employee.

Another letter was sent to the employees on the 18th. May 1984:

Dear Employee,
I wrote to you on the 16th. March 1984 explaining the serious position Purnell and Sons Limited was in and how important it was to achieve a speedy and successful conclusion to the negotiations with employees and their trade union representatives. I know what a shock it must have been to you and the members of your family but a company the size of Purnells can only continue if its operations allow it to compete successfully in this country and abroad.

The losses the Company have been incurring are so heavy that I had no alternative but to write to you to give 90 days notice of closure of the Company on 14th. June 1984, as the progress of those negotiations was totally unsatisfactory.

Negotiations have now resumed and I hereby confirm that the notice given to you and to other employees is rescinded.

Only rapid conclusion of the negotiations can guarantee the £17.2 million proposed investment and secure jobs and the future of Purnells.

I hope you will join with me in doing everything possible to ensure Purnells survival.

Yours sincerely,

P.A. Lavington
Deputy Chief Executive

Another letter followed, dated the 30th.May 1984, headed, 'Is Purnells to be re-equipped to meet the challenges of the 1980's and 1990's, or is it to remain as it is for as long as there is work to keep it going?'

A letter, dated 22nd. June 1984, from Mr. Lavington to the employees followed:

Dear Colleague,
                    In my letter to you of 30th.May 1984, I told you that all our colleagues working at Purnells have a clear and urgent choice to make-that choice is:

1   To reach immediate and final agreements that will enable the Company to re-equip with a major capital investment programme costing £17.2 million, desperately needed for Purnell to be able to handle

substantial British Mail Order Catalogue business, most of which will be bought back from abroad, and to handle magazine publishing such as the Radio Times and Woman and to retain the Observer Colour Magazine, Reader's Digest, etc. and to attract and hold new magazine work.

2   If that investment plan went forward, the Company was ready to bring in modern binding lines as well as a major new 2.4 metre gravure press and two additional web-offset presses. This additional equipment would have provided immediately an increased number of jobs, from the present 546 to 608, notwithstanding the fact that there would be 60-70 voluntary redundancies on most generous tax-free terms.

3   We offered training facilities without loss of pay. Because the new pre-press technology requires fewer people this results in a need for some 60-70 voluntary redundancies and in order to make it attractive for people to accept, we have agreed to pay £900 per year of service. This is of course very generous. In spite of the fact that agreement had not been finalised, as a gesture of goodwill, we have released last Friday, the last of the 29 people each of whom left with an average payment per man, tax free.

4   The urgency of the matter arises from the fact that the Radio Times is switching over from letterpress to web-offset and the last pre-print will be printed at Purnell on August 16th., being the issue dated 23rd.August 1984. Purnell have an order to print one million copies of the web-offset edition, but if there is no agreement with the unions on pay and conditions, then obviously the investment cannot go ahead and the million copies will be printed, by BPPC, elsewhere. Equally, we have orders for mail order catalogues and other commercial

work which the publishers will not place with Purnell if we do not have agreement with the unions to operate the new equipment and to accept outside positives, as do all our competitors for this work, at home and abroad.

5   The urgency cannot be overstated. We have already lost more time than we could possibly afford. It takes time to install the new equipment and to make it operational.

6   As a result of my letter, the SOGAT and NGA chapels held their respective meetings and the Company has been informed as follows:

a)   <u>N.G.A.</u>
        Mr. Alf Parrish, National Secretary of the NGA, has informed us that the NGA chapels have rejected the Company's proposals and cannot agree on the purchase or supply of positives from outside sources.
        Furthermore, the NGA chapels have been applying illegal sanctions against the Company in that they have refused to run the No.6 Cerrutti as a 13-unit press even though it has been ready for full production for the past four weeks. They have also threatened further Industrial Action if the No.1 and No.2 minders differentials are not increased on the implementation of the National Award, despite the express agreement with the NGA National Secretary and the Bristol Branch.

b)   <u>SOGAT</u>
        Mr. John Moakes, National Officer, has informed the Company that the SOGAT chapels have accepted the Company's proposals, in

principal, subject to clarification of minor operational details.

7 Since our customers work cannot be fulfilled unless all the unions working at Purnell accept a settlement on which our investment programme can go forward, the NGA chapel's decision effectively torpedoes the investment plans for Purnell and at the same time kills any chances for increased job opportunities or for the payment of the very generous voluntary redundancy terms that the Company had offered.

Woman

As you will know, owing to the NUJ strike action at IPC, this publication has been suspended. As we have been unable to reach agreement with the unions to modernise Purnell, IPC will not leave Woman at Purnell and it will , therefore return to Watford as soon as publication is resumed.

8 What work is there left for Purnell to do and for how long?

Observer Colour Magazine

The Sunday Telegraph Magazine, moved from gravure at Bemrose to web-offset at Ben Johnson, York, giving the Sunday Telegraph considerable economies and production advantages. The Observer magazine cannot stay at Purnell without new technology and the acceptance of outside positives and, therefore, will be going elsewhere, where the chapels are more appreciative that it is the customer who, in the end, helps to pay their wages.

Reader's Digest

A strong marketing minded company that insists that it's printer provides them with every advantage of modern printing technology and they will accept nothing less. So once more, this magazine cannot be retained without modernisation and there are many printers who would love to take on the job.

Mail order Catalogue Work

Argos was only retained by the skin of our teeth because the customer was made nervous by the process chapel on the question of whether they would or would not handle outside positives for this job and they only said yes at absolutely the last moment. It cannot stay with Purnell next time round, bearing in mind the process chapels refusal to handle outside positives for the Marshall Ward catalogue which was severely delayed, and the J.D. Williams catalogue which had to be printed by one of our competitors. Mail Order Catalogue owners have told me that a work force that tries to dictate, in 1984, where a customer gets his positives done, clearly treats customers with contempt and cannot be trusted with work that Mail Order Catalogue customers can place elsewhere without any difficulty.

Time has run out. If the NGA do not have a change of mind within days rather than weeks, then discussions must immediately take place as to how the Company will now survive on the available work and how many jobs can be saved and for how long?

Yours sincerely,

P.A. Lavington
Chief Executive

P.S. Since dictating this letter, we have suffered irresponsible action by NGA in pursuance of their claim, the possibility of which I referred to in paragraph 6a. Action, which could have serious consequences for the Company. Fortunately common sense has prevailed and normal working has now been resumed.

CHAPTER THIRTEEN

STRIKES, PICKETS AND MANAGEMENT MOVES

The second half of the 1980's was disruptive for both the Book Production factory and the Gravure Factory. Both sides had been pressurized to make savings, which inevitably meant staff reductions, plus increases in productivity in the book production side, without the benefit of the latest equipment and machinery, in order to compete with competition from Europe and the Far East for books and from European gravure competition on magazines and catalogue printing. In the book factory, both the Works Director and the Commercial Director had left for other positions, in the early 1980's, the former as Works Director of Waterlows and the latter to a publishing company in the USA. On the gravure side, in 1986, more demands for savings, in other words staff reductions, were made which led to industrial action, the like of which had not been seen in the printing trade since the 1959 general printing strike.

Mr. John Hart was now the chief executive of Purnell Gravure and of Odhams-Sun, BPPC's other large gravure works, at Watford, in January 1986. It was in January 1986 that more demands for staff reductions were made, from 543, down to 358, a loss of 185 jobs. Notice of a 90-day consultation period was made by the company to conform to the current legislation, which many concluded would mean closure of the factory on the 4th. April 1986 if agreement was not achieved. Mr. Hart stated that company was seeking to change working practices to make Purnell more competitive and to bring the working methods more in line with other British printers.

245

Nearly £20,000,000 had been invested in Purnell since 1984, most of it in the gravure factory. In 1981 650 redundancies had been made, mainly in the book production factory, followed by a further 70, from the gravure site later.

The loss of the contract to print the Observer Colour Magazine, worth some £4 million in 1985, and the failure to replace this lost production, was definitely one of the main reasons to make economies in the gravure sector.

The local chapels (union groups) together with their area union organisers, regarded this latest round of demands, " the straw that broke the camels back", and declared that they had had enough of Maxwell's " bloody Draconian" measures and would fight to the finish, and demanded the withdrawal of 185 redundancy notices.

The local newspapers reported fully on the negotiations week by week, mainly covering the top BPCC management's views and the local unions responses. The strain on the local Managing Directors, and their were several, since the Maxwell involvement, was horrific. Robert Maxwell was an autocratic bully who expected results despite giving out unattainable targets to his subordinates, although he respected the few who stood their ground and put forward logical arguments. By February 1986, another Managing Director of Purnell Gravure, Mr. Brian Wilcox was in the "hot seat" trying his best to achieve a settlement.

On the 7th February, a mass meeting was held by the printers to discuss the latest bombshell dropped by Mr. Maxwell in his letter to employees, stating that the factory was to close on 21st. February with the loss of 544 jobs. The reason given, for this bringing forward of the closure date, so soon after Mr. Hart's statement some three weeks previously, that closure was not even being considered, was that the decline in profits for 1986 was likely to be an enormous £6 million. The result of this action was a strengthening of resolve of the printers to fight to the bitter end. At a meeting held in London, in mid February, between Mr. Maxwell and the trade unions, Mr. Maxwell declared that he wanted Purnells open subject to the economics of running it. At this stage, Purnell Book Production and the Book Service Centre were not under threat of closure.

The haggling continued unabated by both sides and industrial action in the form of picketing by the NGA in early April took place. A rift between NGA and SOGAT was averted on the picket line when the company advised SOGAT to remain at home.

Another strange event happened in early 1986 concerning the control of expenditure on the gravure factory's capital spending programme. After Mr. Wood, the financial director, had left the company at the end of January, some time later, three managers were temporarily removed from their managerial roles, whilst an investigation took place as to why the capital expenditure budget of £22 million had been exceeded by £3 million. The three managers returned to their managerial positions in early March 1986, their characters and that of Mr. Woods, unblemished, however, the company soon found itself somewhat short of good technical managers.

By the 17th. April 1986, the Book Production Plant was now under threat of closure if a plan giving cost savings of £200,000 per year was not received by April 28th. when a 90-day notice of closure would be issued. There were 229 people employed in the book factory. The company had suggested that the savings could be realised by not paying the National Pay Award. The 46 strong, Book Production NGA chapel told Mr. Terry Ulrick, the managing director, that there was no deal.

The general secretary of the NGA, Tony Dubbins, met with Mr. Maxwell, on May 1st. when Mr. Maxwell put forward several points that he considered would be a basis for ending the dispute, which included a pay increase but still required 66 redundancies. Mr. Maxwell set a deadline for noon on the 3rd May, subsequently extended to midnight. The NGA chapels unanimously rejected the proposals at a meeting held to discuss the latest developments.

The gravure factory had by this time, May 3rd., been on strike since the 4th. April when they were considered to have sacked themselves, and not a single sheet of paper had been printed, and the factory was devoid of orders.

The Book Production factory had now received 30 days notice that the pre-press and press department was to close with the loss of 42 jobs. Mr. Maxwell had issued a statement to the union officers that he regretted this action especially as SOGAT, the AEUW, and the EEPTU, had agreed to cost cutting proposals, but regretfully, the NGA chapel had rejected them.

The NGA pickets stopped lorries from entering the premises when non-union drivers were involved, for the first time since the pickets were posted, to prevent paper being transferred to other BPPC printing houses.

Some of the NGA strikers and their representatives travelled to Nottingham to seek co-operation from colleagues at Chromoworks Ltd., another BPCC company. A printed handbill was distributed stating that 185 NGA members of the Purnell chapel had been fired for not accepting compulsory redundancies, the non payment of the 1986 pay award, cuts in holiday pay and a longer working week. It requested colleagues to obey instructions from the union's national council and not to handle work on Woman, Woman and Home, the Radio Times editions for the west country, the south west and Wales, the Reader's Digest magazine and Cable Vision.

On the following Wednesday, the 27th. April, Mr. Hart wrote to the NGA members saying that the handbill was a flagrant misinterpretation of the facts. The main one being the loss of the Observer magazine on pricing, therefore, the company had to reduce the workforce at Purnell Gravure by 185 staff in order to save 544 jobs. Other points were made in the letter and it ended by posing the question, " the largest print union SOGAT has voted to accept these terms. Why not the NGA?" So the exchange of points and counter points continued with neither side yielding, through May and June, until the 27th June, when the 32 electricians and engineers negotiated a return to work document, should the company reopen.

Prince Charles was due to arrive in Paulton on Friday the 11th. July, to open the Business Advice Centre at the Wansdyke Enterprise Agency; the agency is situated in a building provided by Mr. Maxwell's BPCC near to the Purnell works entrance No.4. The Purnell strike was now in it's 14th week and the NGA chapels thought a demonstration for the benefit of Prince Charles would be a good thing, especially so, to quote Mr. John Wiggins, one of two NGA f.o.c.'s at Purnells, "After all 40 people were sacked from that very spot from the Western Ink factory, where the Enterprise Agency now stands and as Prince Phillip and Prince Charles often speak to leaders of industry and encourage support and mutual co-operation, which implies agreements and working arrangements being mutually honoured, which is not the case here.

A month later, August 14th. Tony Dubbins, the NGA general secretary and Robert Maxwell met yet again to arrive at a peace deal for Purnells. Mr. Dubbins carried the Purnell NGA chapel's directive that no compulsory redundancies would be entertained, at least until March 1987. The company wanted 75 redundancies now, still with the other cutbacks in place.

Eventually Mr. Maxwell made the trip to Purnells at Paulton, on the 14th. October, a week after the dispute was settled, albeit uneasily, after 26 weeks of severe industrial unrest. Mr. Maxwell said that some large contracts were coming back to Purnells, such as Radio Times and the Reader's Digest magazine, furthermore, his son Mr. Ian Maxwell, BPPC's marketing and customer relations director, had just obtained an order from a German mail–order firm, the first for many years, and he would like to introduce him to the workforce.

Approximately 160 jobs were lost, leaving about 400, at the conclusion of the negotiations. "I've come to heal the wounds and to reassure them of my personal support and commitment, and to seek their assurances and commitment to the policy that the customer is king and that management manages," he said to the workforce." I have been extremely well received and have been given those assurances, and I feel satisfied that Purnell can look forward to a profitable, expanding and secure future. It is one of the best equipped factories in the British Printing and Communications Corporation."

Mr. Maxwell continued, "We are definitely equipping presses now so that in about three months time we can print colour pages of newspapers. We have orders for our papers to come to Purnell." Mr. Maxwell was now head of the Mirror Group of newspapers.

When Robert Maxwell, in 1981, took control of BPC as it was then, the equity market capitalisation of the company was £13.7 million. On October 1st. 1986 BPCC, as it now was, the capitalisation stood at £656 million.

The toll on the senior management at Purnells continued under the continuous pressure, strain and future uncertainty. Terry Ulrick, the Managing Director of Purnell Book Production Ltd., left for pastures new and Varyl Chamberlain joined the company as Managing Director in November 1986. In 1987 John Raine, previously the Personnel Director of the company, was made Works Director of Purnell Book Production Ltd., he had been with the company since 1958 and had a background in personnel and industrial relations matters. Mick Miller was transferred from the Waterlow factory at Dunstable, where he was the Bindery Manager, to perform the same function at Purnell Book Production.

The 1987-phased budget for the book production factory was to show a loss of £655,000 for the year and the envelope factory, a loss of £25,000 on the management accounts. The prediction taken by the senior management of BPCC in September 1987 was that a statutory profit of £134,000 would be made and a management loss of £700.000, for the book side and a break-even prediction for the envelope factory, or the costs associated with it could be let go. The heavy discounting of prices that took place earlier in 1987 was the reason for the poor results and it was also felt that the number of indirect staff to direct staff was too heavy, using the old formulae of three indirects to one direct. It was clear that the book factory could not continue along it's present lines and several options were considered and evaluated, including closure and transferring £8.5 million of sales to the Aylesbury factory of Hazell Watson & Viney Ltd., and even a M.B.O. (Management Buy Out) by Varyl Chamberlain and John Raine was considered.

This proposed sale was progressed almost to completion, but last minute differences of opinion between the two sides, caused it to fail. Briefly, Mr. Chamberlain's vehicle for buying Purnell Book Production Ltd., was a company he had formed called Quayshelfco 224 Ltd. The principle terms proposed by BPCC for the sale of assets were: Cash-£875,000 and Convertible Subordinated Loan Notes £2,554,000 totalling £3,429,000. The valuation was based on the value of the Sales Assets at 31st. March 1988, which was £ 3,429, 000 from the MIS report. The cash portion of the consideration had been reduced by £50,000 from £925,000 to £875,000 by Kevin Maxwell to compensate Mr. Chamberlain for the potential loss of 5% of the equity arising from the future conversion at BPCC's option of the Loan Notes.

The Loan Notes were to be issued at a par value of 2.5p and a premium of 97.5p. Interest to be paid at 6% per annum. The loan notes would be convertible into 5% of the equity of Quayshelfco 224 Ltd. in 1996, or replaced at par at BPCC's option.

Quayshelfco was to set up an approved pension scheme within 12 months and the transfer value to be calculated by BPCC's actuaries and will include a pension holiday of one year which has been agreed between Mr. Chamberlain and Kevin Maxwell.

The new company would have occupied the same premises under a lease agreement, which was outside the Landlord and Tenants Act, of £98,000 per annum, for up to three years. The lease covered the provision of site services such as telephones, electricity, security etc., up to the end of June 1989, after which the company would have had to make its own arrangements.

The negotiations were deadlocked over the terms of the Loans Notes Instrument concerning the interest payable each year. The rent payable was also a problem, as not all the space currently occupied by the company was being made available by BPCC.

Robert Maxwell and Varyl Chamberlain met over the weekend 30th July 1988 and the purchase price was confirmed at £925,000 with the details to be agreed between Kevin Maxwell and Varyl Chamberlain on the 3rd. August 1988.

Had the two sides have been able to agree terms, the new company would probably have been called International Book Production Ltd., but agreement was not reached and it was back to 'square one' for the book production plant.

The next big surprise occurred on December 22nd 1988, when the corporate finance business of Samuel Montagu & Co. Limited issued a press statement as follows:

MAXWELL COMMUNICATION CORPORATION plc ("MCC")

Proposed sale of BPCC to its management

- MCC announces the proposed sale of its UK commercial printing interests ("BPCC") to Bucksmere Limited ("Bucksmere") for an initial cash consideration of approximately £265 million.
- MCC will retain properties valued by the directors at £30.4 million, net of BPCC's relocation costs.
- MCC will retain certain printing businesses, formerly operated as part of BPCC, with net assets, as at 31st December 1987, of £6.3 million.

- The above arrangements place a value of approximately £301 million on the whole of MCC's UK commercial printing interests.
- Up to a further £30 million consideration could become payable to MCC, contingent on certain future events.
- Bucksmere is a new company formed by the senior management of BPCC and a syndicate of institutional investors.
- The management team is led by Mr. John Holloran, Executive Vice-Chairman and Chief Executive (UK Printing) of MCC.
- MCC will subscribe £21.6 million for Bucksmere share capital, convertible into up to 24.7 per cent. Of Bucksmere's equity on its sale or listing.
- A circular to MCC shareholders will be despatched shortly convening an Extraordinary General Meeting to approve the sale.

Commenting on the proposed sale, Mr. Robert Maxwell, the Chairman of MCC said today:

"The sale of BPCC, which we have successfully built up over the last seven years, is a further major landmark in our transition to a leading international communications and publishing group. The proceeds of the sale will be used to reduce our borrowings and thus will form an important step towards Macmillan's and OAG's consolidation in MCC's balance sheet."

"We decided that BPCC required for its further expansion a considerable commitment of MCC's management and financial resources, which would have been disproportionate in the context of our increased focus on communications and publishing businesses. I am confident that, under John Holloran's dedicated leadership, BPCC will continue to prosper and that our investment in it will reinforce trading links which will remain very important for both groups in the future."

Note: The above headlines must be read in conjunction with the attached full text announcement

Introduction

The Board of MCC announces that it has entered into agreements to sell BPCC to Bucksmere Limited ("Bucksmere"), a company formed by the senior management of BPCC led by Mr. John Holloran who is Executive Vice-Chairman and Chief Executive (UK Printing) of MCC. Under the terms of the sale, MCC will receive approximately £265 million in cash, and will retain certain properties and businesses hitherto forming part of BPCC's operations. These arrangements place a value of approximately £301 million on the whole of the UK commercial printing interests of MCC. Furthermore, deferred consideration of up to £30 million could be payable if Bucksmere were to sell certain companies and businesses, and on a sale or listing of Bucksmere.

As part of these arrangements, MCC also will subscribe £26.6 million for share capital in Bucksmere which, on a sale or listing of Bucksmere, could result in MCC holding up to a maximum of 24.7% of Bucksmere's then issued ordinary share capital.

Details of the proposed sale

Under the terms of the sale, the initial consideration to be receivable by MCC is £264.6 million in cash, including the settlement of inter-company loan accounts, subject to adjustment in respect of net assets. Deferred consideration of up to £10 million could become payable if Bucksmere sells certain companies and businesses forming part of BPCC, and further deferred consideration of up to £20 million could become payable if the value of Bucksmere, on its sale or listing, exceeds certain predetermined amounts. The Board of Bucksmere has stated that it intends to seek a listing for Bucksmere's share capital on The Stock Exchange within five years.

MCC will retain title to various properties, hitherto part of BPCC's operations, and which have a current book value of £16.3 million. The Board of MCC estimates that these properties have a current market value of £35.8 million, but believes that an amount in excess of this could be realised were they to be redeveloped. MCC has agreed to grant Bucksmere short leases, ranging from 12 to 30 months, on a number of these properties in order to allow Bucksmere sufficient time to relocate the affected operations. MCC has agreed to compensate Bucksmere for consequential relocation costs of up to a maximum of £5.4 million. The remaining properties are not required by Bucksmere and are now vacant or let to third parties. On Achieving vacant possession, MCC intends to sell or redevelop all these properties.

MCC will also retain certain printing businesses, formerly operated as part of BPCC, which achieved operating profits of £1.0 million in 1987 and had net assets of £6.3 million as at 31st. December 1987.

The effect of the arrangements outlined above is therefore to place a value, exclusive of any deferred consideration, of approximately £301 million on the whole of the UK commercial printing interests of MCC, made up as to £264.6 million cash proceeds on the sale of BPCC, £30.4 million in the value of remaining properties after relocation costs and £6.3 million in the asset value of retained businesses.

As part of these arrangements, MCC will enter into agreements with Bucksmere for the provision by Bucksmere of printing services to MCC.

Reasons for the proposed sale

Announcements have already been made in relation to the successful $2.6 billion offer for Macmillan, and the proposed $750 million acquisition of OAG. These transactions are being effected through off-balance sheet companies and the Board of MCC expects Macmillan and OAG to become members of the MCC group during 1989.

The acquisitions of these two major US publishing businesses represent a major strategic refocusing of the MCC group's businesses in the publishing and communications arena on both sides of the Atlantic. Against this background, the Board decided to sell BPCC so as to free the substantial managerial and financial resources, which MCC would otherwise have had to devote to BPCC over the next few years. In taking this decision, the Board determined that the price and terms negotiated should properly reflect BPCC's prospects and should be consistent with the interests of the business and its employees.

To build on the foundations laid over the last seven years, the Board of MCC now believes that there is a need for BPCC to carry out a further significant capital expenditure programme if it is to maintain its leading position in the commercial printing industry against the increasing competition which can be expected in the European printing market in the years ahead. The effects of these increasing competitive pressures were key to the Board's assessment of the future prospects of BPCC within MCC. In these circumstances the Board of MCC believes that BPCC can best meet this challenge under new ownership with a specialist and dedicated management team.

The proceeds of the sale will be used to reduce the group's borrowings and will thus form an important step towards achieving a level of borrowings, which will allow Macmillan and OAG to be consolidated into MCC's balance sheet without breaching the various borrowing restrictions to which MCC is subject.

Information on BPCC

The origins of BPCC lie within the group of printing companies, which has developed directly since 1981 out of the British Printing Corporation Limited, which was rescued in that year from imminent receivership by Pergamon Press Limited under the Chairmanship of Mr. Robert Maxwell. The outstanding success of the business rationalisation and financial reconstruction plan, which was then carried out, has enabled the businesses to develop into the substantial group seen today.

BPPC now comprises approximately 40 operating companies and businesses, employing approximately 7,100 people. It is divided into four main divisions:

- Magazines and catalogues
- Security and corporate printing
- Books and journals
- Specialist packaging and labelling

The magazines and catalogues division is one of the largest magazine and catalogue printers in the UK and has printing facilities utilising the gravure, heatset web offset and coldest web offset methods.

The security and corporate printing division is involved in the printing of financial and corporate documents, cheques and credits, plastic cards, business forms, direct marketing material and other general documents.

The books and journals division, typesets, prints and binds, hardback books, paperback books, limp bound books and numerous specialist journals.

The specialist packaging and labelling division manufactures and prints, folding cartons and wet glue labels. It also prints and distributes calendars, distributes bar-coding equipment and manufactures self- adhesive on-roll labels.

In the year to 31st. December 1987, BPCC achieved profits of £29.4 million, before tax and after the benefit of a pension contribution holiday, on a turnover of £290.6 million. As at 31st. December 1987, it had attributable net assets of £177.3 million.

Information on Bucksmere and MCC's proposed investment

Bucksmere is a newly incorporated company formed for the purpose of acquiring BPCC by members of the senior management of BPCC as well as certain institutional investors.

The Chief Executive of Bucksmere will be Mr. John Holloran and the Chairman will be Mr. Michael Stoddart, who is Chairman of Electra Investment Trust.

The other executive directors of Bucksmere will be Mr. John Ashfield, Mr. Jim Brown Mr. Geoff Garwood, Mr. Anthony Gordon and Mr. John Hart, all of whom are directors of companies within BPCC. On completion of the sale, Mr. Holloran will resign as a director of MCC and the other executive directors of Bucksmere will resign from their executive positions in the MCC group. MCC will have the right to appoint a non-executive director to the Board of Bucksmere, and intends to nominate Mr. Ian Maxwell.

MCC has agreed to subscribe £21.6 million for Bucksmere shares which on Bucksmere's sale or listing would represent a maximum of 24.7 per cent. Of Bucksmere's then issued share capital.

The Board also believes that the proposed subscription for Bucksmere share capital provides an excellent long-term investment opportunity for MCC, in a business it knows well, with management for whom it has a high regard and which will be a significant supplier of print to the MCC group in the future.

Extraordinary General Meeting

In view of the size of the proposed transaction, and the interest of Mr. Holloran and the management of BPCC in Bucksmere, the proposed sale will be conditional upon the approval of ordinary shareholders of MCC. A circular setting out the details of the proposed sale and containing notice of an Extraordinary General Meeting, at which an ordinary resolution to approve the sale will be proposed, will be despatched to MCC shareholders as soon as possible.

Completion of the proposed sale is expected to take place as soon as possible after shareholder approval has been obtained.

MCC was advised on this transaction by Samuel Montagu & Co. Limited.

As far as Purnells was concerned, the clause relating to retained businesses was to have a later impact, in relation to the Purnell Service Centre, which remained in the MCC group and whose staff suffered great anxiety over their pension expectations.

It should be noted that John Holloran negotiated, successfully the transfer of the BPCC pension fund out of MCC, before the well-publicised pension scandal emerged.

The financial press, in January 1992, reported that when Mr. Holloran took BPCC out of MMC, there were some 4,000-pension fund members. Nearly £100 million was owed to the BPCC pension scheme and this was successfully transferred to the fund in late September and early October 1991. The money arrived safely at the very time when the Maxwell empire was under its most extreme financial pressure.

Under the buyout agreement an initial £30 million went into the BPPC pension fund and a further £97 million was due last autumn, when the money several weeks late, Mr. Holloran, who is chairman of the pension fund, contacted Mr. Maxwell and £50 million arrived in late September while the balance was paid in early October. "All our pension money has been paid over. It's virtually all in alpha shares, cash or gilts," said Mr. Holloran.

Back at Paulton, at factory level, some rationalisation was taking place; two BPCC companies and one MCC Company, the Book Service Centre, now occupied the Paulton site.

The Reader's Digest magazine, printed by the gravure factory, was you will recall, sent each month, to Hazell Watson and Viney Ltd., a member of BPCC and part of the Book Production Group, for binding and despatching by post. The distance between the two factories was a little over a 100 miles and the transport cost was something that the company could well do without. On the 24th. July 1989, a meeting was held at Aylesbury, with the customer to discuss the practicality of binding and dispatching the RDA magazine at Paulton, right next-door to where it was printed, by Paulton Book Production Ltd.

At this meeting were, representing the Reader's Digest Association, David Richards, Eve Saddler (Distribution), and Roland Reynolds, (Production Manager). Representing BPCC were Michael Pegge (Chairman of the Book Production Group), Terry Goodman (Director and General Manager of HWV), Roy Southam (HWV Customer Relations Manager), and John Raine (Works Director Purnell). The meeting agreed that the transfer was a good idea and would benefit the Book Production Factory by giving it regular work each month, and that one Sheridan Perfect Binding Machine and a Sitma Mailing machine be transferred from Aylesbury to Paulton with the November 1989 issue being produced as a split production run between Aylesbury and Paulton.There were a few start-up problems, all overcome, and the complete production was soon being achieved at Paulton. The proximity of modern, fast running perfect-binding machines also improved the gravure factory's standing in acquiring print and bind orders such as the Argos catalogue.

There was a tragic accident in the gravure factory during April 1989 when Steve Comer, 33 years old, was killed after becoming entangled in a packaging machine.

In the early hours of November 5th. 1991, at 4.25 am, to be precise, Robert Maxwell was seen walking on the deck of his yacht, Lady Ghislaine, by a crewmember. At 9.45 am, the Lady Ghislaine anchored off the harbour of Los Christianos in Tenerife. A call was put through to Mr. Maxwell's cabin at 11.0am, but he could not be found, an alarm was raised and a sea search began. The Madrid Air Sea Rescue reported finding his body at 5.46 pm November 5th 1991, floating some 20 miles off Gran Canaria.

The following day the world's international press carried the news on their headlines, and speculation was rife, as to the cause of Mr. Maxwell's death. The preliminary findings of a post-mortem held on the 6th. November showed that he had died of a heart attack. There was not enough water in the deceased's lungs for death to have been caused by drowning. Robert Maxwell was buried in Jerusalem on the Mount of Olives on November 10th. 1991.

By early December 1991, accountants found that maybe up to four fifths of the assets of the Mirror Group Newspapers pension fund was missing; Mr. Maxwell during the summer months had withdrawn about £400 million without authority, leaving the fund short of some £175 million to meet all its liabilities. The serious fraud office was called in. The rest of the story has been well-documented elsewhere and needs not to be repeated here except to say that the Paulton Service Centre staff suffered anxiety for many months concerning the future of their MCC pensions.

At the Book Production factory in late 1991, John Raine was appointed General Manager, John had been previously the Works Director and before that the Personnel Director.

Varyl Chamberlain had left the Company, after a disagreement with the CEO and went to another book producing firm on the south coast.

Robert Maxwell, a complicated man who could rightly claim to be, a war hero, a genius, a bully, a risk taker and in the final analysis a dishonest man.

It cannot be denied that he saved BPC in 1981 from financial disaster and disintegration.

His tough cost saving exercises across BPC fell no heavier than at Paulton, an exercise that the work force never forgot, particularly in the years immediately ahead.

The manner of his demise remains a mystery, speculation in the Press covered assassination, murder, accident and suicide. I like to think he took his own life, he was a brave man and had proved it in the army, he must have known that his risky misdemeanours would be shortly revealed and the public shame was too much for him to face.

He was a large, colourful man, whose shadow, some felt, had loomed over Paulton far too long. One thing is certain; he will not be forgotten easily.

Michael Pegge had been a management trainee at Hazell Watson & Viney Ltd., the well-known book printers and binders in Aylesbury Buckinghamshire. Latterly he had held the positions of Commercial Director of Hazells Offset at Slough and Managing Director of Waterlows at Dunstable before joining the corporate staff at Maxwell House and finally Managing Director of Hazell Watson and Viney Ltd. and Chairman of the Book Production Group.

Michael Pegge, chairman of the Book Production Group, which included Purnell
(Book Production) Ltd.

The Purnell team are pictured from number five, left to right, Terry Goodman Works Director, Tony Wilmott Printing Manager, Chris Andrews Production Manager and Keith Brown Managing Director.

Although Purnells was recognised throughout the printing trade as children's book producers, they also had experience in financial printing. For over 21 years Purnells produced the Annual Report and Account for the Royal Dutch Shell petroleum company. Pictured here, at the Shell headquarters, is the Purnell Production Team of four, slightly outnumbered by their Shell friends in 1981.

Every year, whilst the Report and Account was in production, a team of Shell executives visited the Purnell factory and lived with the job until it was finally dispatched.

In 1994 Purnell's parent company changed its name, yet again, from the British Printing and Communication Corporation to The British Printing Company Ltd. with effect from 1st. February.

CHAPTER FOURTEEN

THE END OF CASED-BOOK PRODUCTION

The dismantling of the elements on the Purnell site in particular and the group in general, was a slow business, the first on-site business to go was the Western Ink Company, which was sold to the Fishburn Printing Ink Company on 11th. January 1984, who were to consolidate it into their own facilities. The old boot factory, which had housed the manufacturing unit, was vacated and also the new office building, opposite was made available for letting.

The old Litho plate making and press room area, which had been vacated in the 1981 re-organisation of Book Production, and subsequently filled with bound-book storage racking for Futura Publishing, was again cleared to house a new bindery to perfect bind magazines and catalogues. This bindery was to come under the management of the gravure Division and to compliment their wire stitch and trim bindery. To facilitate this move, the old Sheridan Rack-Drive perfect binder from Hazell Watson and Viney Ltd. was transferred to Paulton and the Readers Digest perfect binder, a fast running Sheridan machine, moved down from the Book Production site.

The M.A.N. web-offset press No.3 had already been dismantled, moved over to the Gravure site, overhauled and re-erected near to the gravure presses.

It should not be forgotten that Purnells, under the Clifford Purnell and Wilfred Harvey management control, had over the years built up a considerable amount of land and property in and around Paulton. This property was disposed of by successive managements that followed them; perhaps a case of selling the family silver.

Rosewell Farm at High Littleton, about 144 acres, was bought in1942 from Walter Austin Panes, in the usual secretive manner of doing business at that time, Purnells used Wilfred Harvey's daughter's name on the deeds, Betty Jean Rogers Lavington

. On the 3rd.September 1951, it was transferred to Purnell and Sons Ltd. by a conveyance signed by Betty Jean Rogers Lavington. In 1974 it was sold by BPC to Walter Leonard Heal.

The Down Farm, High Littleton, comprising 73 acres 2roods 3 perches was bought on 29th. September 1943, from Albert Norris Abbot and again Betty Jean Rogers Lavington's name appears on the deed and described as the wife of Peter Lavington at present serving as an aircraftsman in H.M. Services. This property was conveyed to Purnell and Sons on 29th. July 1947. In November 1966 it was sold to the British Printing Corporation and eventually sold piecemeal, with the firm of builders Wimpey, buying 16.57 acres in 1967.

The Edwards Factory in Paulton with land had been purchased by Clifford Purnell in two lots and was transferred to Purnell and Sons Ltd. in 1935 when the limited company was formed. This was sold to that well-known local builder Ken Biggs on 14th. December 1976 for £17,500. The factory had an area of 11,612 sq.ft. and the land just under an acre. Some of this land had previously been sold in 1973 for the Paulton Rovers Supporters Club.

Norton Hill Farm in Midsomer Norton had been bought to build and develop the packaging business of Purnell and Sons, called Runprint, back in the early 1960's. This business and land was sold in 1967.

Purnells also bought 15.75 acres of land at Underhill Lane Midsomer Norton that had belonged to a well-known local character, farmer Charley Fry and his sister Miss F. M. Fry, after their deaths, at an auction held on 21st. September 1955. This land was in the tenancy of

THE END OF CASED-BOOK PRODUCTION

Mr. John Simmons and Purnells needed houses for their staff. In fact by 1968 there was a need for 18 houses to accommodate incoming pre-press and printing operators. This land was developed and, the houses were built and became High Meadows Estate.

On the 12th. November 1995, at a massed meeting, the Purnell Book Production staff was informed that the bindery was to close before Christmas. The blow for the stunned workforce was softened somewhat by the management stating that jobs might be found elsewhere in the BPC group. Printing was to continue at the factory and the sheets sent away for binding. The current Managing Director, Richard Beese said: "Despite the considerable efforts of both management and employees, the bindery has lost money for the last three years. We simply cannot continue to incur these losses, nor can we justify further investment on the back of this performance. Consequently we are intending to close the operation on December 15th. 1995". The factory engaged on book production duly closed.

The records show that book production had always generated profits at Paulton, since 1935 anyway. It was the profits generated from books that financed the installation of the Gravure Department in 1961 and bolstered the Company's and Corporate profits in subsequent years when the gravure and publishing companies were making huge losses. Perhaps the Company never recovered from the decimation of the book production concern in 1981 by Robert Maxwell, when over 800 staff became redundant. It is nice to know that two other local book factories, both as long established as Purnell, namely Butler and Tanner of Frome and The Bath Press have flourished under enlightened management and long may they continue.

The gravure company lost its name in the 1990's from Purnell to Polestar; the name adopted by the group after the departure of John Holloran and this really ends the story, except that Polestar did draw up plans in 1998 for a new printing factory to be built below the old buildings of the 1930's. This factory would have a manufacturing area of over 14,000 sq. mts. with office space of 740 sq.mts; it was submitted for planning permission in May 2002. Will Paulton become another booming printing centre?

CHAPTER FIFTEEN

SPORTS AND SOCIAL OCCASIONS

The Purnell & Sons' Social and Athletic Club, was certainly in existence in 1926, because that is when they formed the Cricket Section. The President was Clifford Purnell, the Honorable Secretary was W. J. Brooks, and the Treasurer was Wilfred Harvey.

On the notice board in 1927 was posted this notice.

NOTICE
PURNELL & SONS' CRICKET CLUB

IT IS PROPOSED – in order to make provision for a properly laid CRICKET PITCH – to accept the offer of MESSRS SUTTON, SEED COMPANY to provide us with a Cricket Pitch 30 yds. X 30 yds. To be ready for the 1930 Cricket Season at a cost of approximately £65.

To raise this money, it is proposed to create a loan of approximately £65, at 6% per annum, to be redeemed by further subscriptions by the Members and also by the help of others who are interested in the Cricket Club and would be so kind to give a Donation.

The following players have kindly consented to raise their subscription per week by the amount shewn against their names and other gentlemen, who are interested in the Cricket, have kindly given Donations as follows: -

DONATIONS

Mr. Purnell	£5. 0. 0.
Mr.Fricker	£1. 0. 0.
Mr. Draper	£- 10. 0.
Mr. Wakeman	£- 5. 0.
Mr. Greathead	£- 7. 6.
Mr. John Brooks	£- 5. 0.
Mr.Savery.	£- 5. 0.

SUBSCRIPTIONS PER WEEK.

Mr. Rawlins.	1/-
Mr. C. Williams	6d.
Mr. W. Brooks	1/-
Mr. F. Shearn	3d.
Mr. F. Brooks.	3d.
Mr. White.	3d.
Mr. Sayers	2d.
Mr. Green.	3d.
Mr. Troake.	3d.
Mr. R. Fear	3d
Mr. Elver.	6d.
Mr. K. Hall.	1d.
Mr. J. Jeffery.	2d.
Mr. T. Briers.	3d.
Mr. A. Stephens	6d.
Mr. C. Shearn	1d.
Mr. T. Rogers.	3d.
Mr. B. Blacker	1d
Mr. W. Harvey	5/-
Mr. L. Marshall	3d.
Mr. R. West	3d.
Mr. E. Ford.	1d.
Mr.S. Evans	1d.
Mr. S. Webb.	6d.
Mr. S. C. Hunt.	6d.

Mr. D. W. Jones.	6d
Mr. J. Carter.	3d.
Mr. W. Carter	3d.

Will other Members and any Gentlemen who would like to help, kindly give their names to MR. W. BROOKS or add their names to the list.

It is proposed, in order to raise the sum necessary, to hold concerts during the next few months, when it is hoped that quite a substantial amount will be raised towards the Fund.

It is to be understood that as soon as the amount necessary has been raised, the additional weekly subscriptions will be discontinued.

Unfortunately, the dance held on the 23rd. November 1928 made a loss of £0-18. 11. as illustrated by Wilfred Harvey's audit of the event, as follows:-

Receipts				Expenditure	
Tickets sold				Mr. Banks	7/2
Mr. Albert Carter	25@ 6d			Rent of Hall	£1
	7@1/-	£0 –19 - 6.		Mrs. Ford	5/-
				Caretaker	2/6
Miss Effie Bourton	6 @ 6d			Tickets	6/6
	1 @ 1/-	£0 - 4 - 0.		Mr. Hooking	8/-
Mr.T.Briers.	2 @ 6d.			Pianist	7/6
	1 @ 1/-	£0 – 2 - 0.		Slipperene	2/-
Mrs. Myrtle Filer	8 @6d			Milk	1/3
	3 @ 1/-	£0 – 7 - 0.			
Mr.J.Brooks	9 @ 6d				
	4 @ 1/-	£0 – 8 - 6.			
Adverse Balance		£0-18-11			
		£2–19-11		£2 –19-11	

Mr. Banks' bill for 7/2 was for groceries supplied from his shop at Park Corner.

Purnell & Sons Cricket Team in 1927 at the Paulto Hill ground.

In the above photograph the following have been identified:- Ivy Carter, Mr. Waine (The firms Travelling Salesman), William Brooks, Frank Brooks, Harold Brooks, W. Shearn, Jack Clements, Mr. Jones, Len Chivers, Mr. Coughlin, Mr. Savery, Mr. C. J. Purnell, Mrs. Watts, Miss Lewis, Cliff Williams, Mr. Fricker, Bert Williams, Wilfred Harvey, Mrs. Maytap and Mrs. May Harvey.

The match was against Highgate Albion Cricket Club from London.

The visitors arrived from London on the Friday night by train; they were met at Bath and conveyed to Paulton by motorcars. The catering on Saturday was in the capable hands of Miss Tapp, Mr. Purnells housekeeper, assisted by the ladies from the committee.

Two matches were played, both games being won comfortably by the stronger, visiting team.
Purnells were dismissed for 20 and 45 runs respectively. During Purnells second innings, Wilfred Harvey was hit on the left cheek by a bouncer and required medical attention. Clifford Purnell drove

Wilfred Harvey to Dr. Crook where it was learned that the left cheek bone was fractured.

The fledgling cricket team played many more interesting games in the 30's on their new ground at Bristol Road Paulton. In 1931 they opened the season with a 59 run win over Stoke St. Michael and later in the season played against Paulton Old Boys, who had for their opening batsman, Clarence Bourton the ex-Bristol City F. C. player and the previous seasons' Blackburn Rovers Centre forward. Purnells won this game, the scores being Purnells 143 and the Old Boys 84. Wilfred Harvey, according to the records, was a very useful bowler, much better than his performances with the bat.

Purnell & Sons cricket club annual dinner in 1936, held in the Lamb Inn, Paulton. In this picture can be seen from left to right S. Mills, Frank Harvey, Cliff Mitcham, Fred Church, Oliver Weeks, Bert Weeks, Bob Payne, Cliff Clarke, Jack Carter, Jack Hookings, Ron Tucker, Horace Prew, Ron Francis, Wilf Shearn, Cliff Williams, Cecil Wych, Eddie Hounsel, Mr. Hobbs (School Master), Dave Flint, Len Haul, R. A. Ingle (Somerset C.C. Captain), Wilfred Harvey (Managing Director of Purnells), L. Carter and W. Brown.

The captain of the cricket team, up to 1936 was Wilfred Harvey; from 1936 it was Eddie Hounsel. Eddie had joined the company in 1934 as an account executive and he enjoyed his cricket as wicket keeper in his leisure time. Eddie had a trial for Somerset County, as wicket keeper at the peak of his playing career and for many years was the fixtures secretary for Purnell C.C., even after his retirement.

Purnell's Ladies Cricket Team in 1937

Shown in this picture are, back row, left to right, Emmie Sperring, Mrs. Platts, Tessie Wall, Doris Church, Winnie Harvey, Mona Seaford, Beryl Plumley, front row, unidentified, Margaret Howell, Marjorie Lewis, Miss Morris (Mrs. Stock), Queenie Hillman.

Winnie Harvey was Bert Harvey's daughter, Mona Seaford became the personnel manager of the company, Miss Morris and Queenie Hillman took care of the secretarial duties of the directors.

It is not recorded if the Ladies ever challenged the Gentlemen to a game.

The cricket teams (there were now two) continued to prosper, even though the war years made things impossible, but after the war a big expansion and interest in games took place.

In 1948, Purnells held the first Flower Show and Sports Day combined, on their Sports Ground, it was estimated that about a 1,000 people attended. The first Sports Day held by Purnells was in 1932.

It was the first sports day held since the war and the first time ever to have a flower show combined with it. The event was organised by a small committee chaired by Mr. R F Franks. Mrs. Wilfred Harvey presented the prizes and the managers and directors officiated as judges and starters, for which they were thanked by Mr. Franks at the conclusion of the events. The silver challenge cup, given by the board of directors, for the department that had won the most points, was presented to Mr.R.J.S.Howell, in charge of the cutting room, which had collected 31.5 points, the office team came second with 30 points. Mr. E. R. Curtis won the Flower Show Challenge Cup, Miss Eileen Bull won the Ladies Tennis Cup, Maurice Harvey won the Men's Tennis Cup, the engineering department won the Mile Relay Cup and the Creech St. Michael Paper Mill team won the Tug-of-War Cup.

The 1950 Sports Day: Some of the officials, the man in the trilby was Bertram Clarke, the Company Secretary and in the white coat, Mr. Pearmain of BPE.

This popular event continued as an annual show for several years, enjoying good weather with the exception of 1953 when the event was practically wiped out by heavy rain.

The Purnell football team for the 1938 season. Pictured are: B. Pitney, H. Woodland, T. Bull, J. Young, J. Illes, K. Sage, R. Carter, L. Woolfrey, B. Hobbs, T. Manley and Ken Wright.

Apart from football and cricket, Purnells also fielded men's and women's hockey teams, tennis and bowls followed, and skittles became extremely popular by both men and women, eventually leading to departmental teams competing in a factory league each year.

Another annual event started in November 1931, and that was the Purnell Social Evening, held under the auspices of the Bristol District Typographical Society. It was held on Thursday 19th. November 1931 in the Church House Paulton and was honoured by guests from the Bristol District Committee of the Joint Industrial Council and the Master Printers Federation. Clifford Purnell also attended and all, including a "meat tea", enjoyed a very entertaining musical evening. These annual evenings continued right up to the outbreak of war and then resumed in 1947.

John Brooks retires as composing room manager, with Wilfred Harvey. Apart from working closely together since 1924, they also were cricketing companions.

Retirements were celebrated departmentally with speeches, the giving of gifts, almost without exception by a company director and the local trade union representative, followed by photographs. A few of these photographs are shown here. In later years the wife of the person retiring was invited too and received flowers from the company.

Several members of the staff completed 50 years service with the company, this included Miss Ivy Carter who carried on working after she had completed her 50 years. Stanley Evans, the manager of the letterpress, black and white section, was another with 50 years service behind him when he retired. Stan joined Purnells on May 7th. 1923 as a letterpress apprentice, he was one of the first to be engaged as an apprentice by the Company. He worked in the letterpress colour room as a machine minder and then became the overseer of that department.

Tom Briers's retirement in 1965. L to R. Ken Bateson, Tom Briers, Stan Evans, Vic Savage and Arthur Cornish.

Fred Shearn's retirement, 28th. July 1967. From L to R. Stan Evans, (Print Manager) Arthur Cornish,(Personnel Director) Fred Shearn, Frank Woodland (Comps Manager) and George Lambert.(FOC Comps.).

Stan Heal's retirement, 8th. Oct. 1965. L to R. Stan Heal (Overseer Monotype Casters), George Lambert (FOC) and Bill Harvey (Managing Director).

Alf Carey on his retirement in 1978 aged 65 years. Manager of the folding Dept.

279

From L to R. Mona Seaford (Personnel Manager), Ernie Langridge, (Folding Room Manager), Roger Trubody (Foreman), Dorothy Taylor, Nancy Edgell, Gerty Beacham and Terry Goodman (Works Director).

Ernie Langridge, the folding room manager, retires in Oct.1984. L to R. Brian Bushell, Terry Goodman, Keith Brown, Ernie Langridge, Mrs. Langridge and Tony Jones.

Charlie Thatcher, maintenance department retires seen with Maurice Harvey.

As the Purnell factory grew on the Paulton site, a site that sloped severely towards the Cam Brook, drainage was of great importance. Charlie Thatcher knew the position of every pipe and drain on the entire site, all from memory.

Maurice Harvey, the chief engineer, was the son of Fred Harvey and Maurice will always be remembered for his love of plants and trees. He was a keen gardener, not only did he keep an immaculate garden of his own at Bloomfield in Bath, but he ensured that the Purnell site was beautifully kept. The front gardens were always a pleasure to see, full of interesting and sometimes unusual shrubs. The Dutch elm disease that decimated the trees on the Paulton site caused Maurice Harvey deep concern. Maurice took over the maintenance department management from Bill Draper and oversaw a lot of development and installations at Purnells that included web-offset printing, the development of the gravure building, boiler house, ink factory and solvent recovery plant, plus several relocation of plant exercises.

The Bindery Ladies Supporters Club. From L to R. Jenny Fooks, Alma Lock, Gwen Fooks, Edie Shearn, Joan Jeffery, Maud Evans and Vi Milsom. Date 1962.

One of the most popular past-times enjoyed by the staff at Purnells, was skittles. The Sports Club had it's own skittle alley as did most of the local public houses. Every department, indeed every section within a department, had its skittle team with a name, such as "The Bindery Belles". The man, who did much of the organising of the matches for many years, even after he had retired, was Cecil Wych.

Every year a Grand Finals play-off was held in the Sports and Social Club with a director of the Company presenting the cups and prizes for the various categories of the skittles competition.

The office skittles team, in the 1970's.
The captain is Eddie Howells-Vaughan standing front centre left and a youthful Miles Gander is seen at the rear, second from the right.

The Married Couples Competition. From L to R. Jack and Joyce Hillman with Joyce and Wilf Roberts from the Bindery Department.

The 1970's were memorable years for the Purnell Cricket Club, in 1974 Tony Barnett made history for the club when he took all ten wickets of the visiting team, Westland Sports and returned figures of 10 for 11 in 11.5 overs.

The Club celebrated it's Golden Jubilee, with a dinner on the 28th.February 1976, and one of the nicest touches of this event was Miss Ivy Carter responding to the toast "The Ladies", Ivy is in the 1927 photograph, third from the left.

The 50 years of Purnell cricket was further celebrated at the annual dinner, held at the Paulton Rovers Club when Mr. Brian Close, the Somerset C.C. Captain gave the 180 guests a witty and entertaining speech.

David Bailey, the Chairman of Purnells Cricket Club, at this time was also the company secretary and a director of Purnell & Sons Ltd.

David enjoyed his cricket and did a lot for the club and other sections of the Sports Club. A chartered accountant, he joined Purnells in 1964 as the assistant accountant, became the secretary in 1966 and a director two years later. During the Maxwell reorganisation, in July 1981, he became Managing Director of the Purnell Publishing Division, then after working for the Company for 20 years Maxwell asked him to resign at 50 years of age. However, David kept his connections with the Cricket Section of the Sports Club and started a new career, locally in publishing.

One of the highlights of David Bailey's cricketing connections with Purnells Cricket Club was at the club's annual dinner and dance in 1977, when he was invited to accept the Presidency of the Somerset Cricket League.

The Purnell XI who played against Peter Robinson's XI in 1972, Peter Robinson was the head of the British Printing Corporation in the 1970's.

In this picture are from left to right, back row, Derek Turner, Gordon Harrington, David Bailey, Chris Lancaster, Bill Kingman, Alex Carey, the umpire is Jack Barwell. Front row: Tony Bray, Mike Jones, Jeff Jones (Captain), Brian Harrington and Geoff Clare.

Purnells won the game by eight wickets.

The fixture with the Head-Office XI became an annual one and Purnells did not always have an easy game as they faced stiffer opposition each year as ex-county players joined the Head-Office team and even non-BPC players. The 1973 match was a good example of this with Chris Greetham, formerly of Somerset, hitting 105 runs out of a total of 221 for the Peter Robinson XI. Bad light came to the aid of Purnells in this match when the game stopped, as Purnells were 130 for 7. David Bailey was the highest scorer for Purnells with 28 not out.

Bill Draper, the retired Chief Engineer and Director of Purnells, with Clifford Purnell on his birthday at Park Corner. Bill was an innovative engineer who modified and invented machines to satisfy customer requirements.

These two grand old men, together, embodied the spirit of Purnells and helped to make it the great company that it was.

APPENDIX ONE

PURNELL'S BINDERY OUTPUTS

Year	Perfect Bound	Cased	Total
1936	2,759,921	7,368,888	10,128,809
1937	5,387,936	8,421,598	13,809,534
1938	8,020,925	8,246,601	16,675,526
1939	6,521,537	8,783,414	15,304,951
1940	3,768,832	6,705,262	10,474,094
1941	1,617,313	6,250,222	7,867,535
1942	778,967	4,761,812	5,540,779
1943	------	6,330,915	6,330,915
1944	------	5,853,294	5,853,294
1945	------	6,682,407	6,682,407
1946	------	8,722,832	8,722,832
1947	------	11,224,611	11,224,611
1948	------	14,040,568	14,040,568
1949	------	12,019,661	12,019,661
1950	1,082,108	13,450,735	14,532,843
1951	653,393	16,754,459	17,407,852
1952	1,133,272	14,820,934	15,954,206
1953	1,242,792	19,313,452	20,556,244
1954	2,702,416	22,424,347	25,126,763
1955	3,054,754	24,071,144	27,575,898
1956	2,178,603	25,929,280	28,107,883
1957	5,294,989	26,584,998	31,879,987
1958	5,911,112	22,804,007	28,715,119
1959	6,041,444	17,699,231	23,740,675
1960	3,584,400	19,835,874	23,420,274
1961	5,396,492	17,896,787	23,293,297
1962	1,381,390	13,750,070	15,131,460
1963	1,314,043	13,729,708	15,043,751
1964	2,979,114	12,318,078	15,297,192
1965	3,386,644	11,709,677	15,096,321
1966	2,236,573	12,648,937	14,885,510

1967	2,095,964	12,805,472	14,901,436
1968	1,255,438	16,513,410	17,768,848
1969	5,836,051	15,979,626	21,815,677
1970	10,094,941	15,804,309	25,899,250
1971	15,058,130	16,137,227	31,195,357
1972	14,848,509	20,716,306	35,564,815
1973	19,493,425	23,458,311	42,951,736
1974	15,887,940	22,575,358	38,463,298
1975	10,706,953	21,263,850	31,970,803
1976	7,320,434	12,910,310	20,230,744
1977	11,766,782	11,364,907	23,131,689
1978	17,496,124	13,150,202	30,646,326
1979	15,266,085	10,685,279	25,951,364
1980	13,390,540	10,649,537	24,040,077

1981: Purnell massive redundancy programme under Robert Maxwell.

APPENDIX TWO

The factory area in the early 1920's.

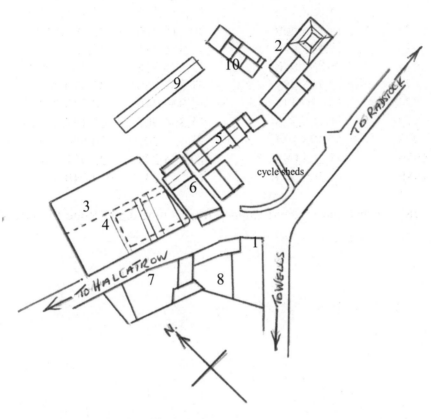

Key to Plan: No.1- Mr. Purnell's house.
No.2- Paulton Manor Farmhouse and outbuildings.
No.3- Two storey, flat roofed building.
No.4- Single storey, ridged roof building with later added inner gallery.
No.5- Single storey, old farm buildings as No.9.
No.6- Single storey, flat roofed and well lit building for colour work.
Nos.7 & 8, the first extensions to the Park Corner premises. No.7 was built on the garden leased from Mr. Purnell's neighbour.
No.10- Old farm buildings.

The 1935 Valuation Plan of Purnells when it became a Public Company

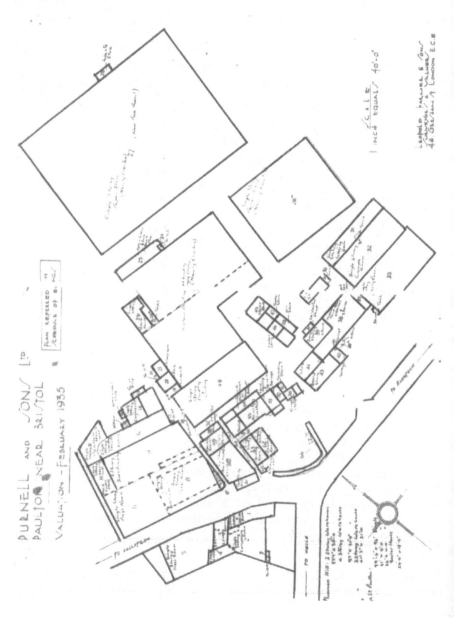

APPENDIX FOUR

The 1943 Air-Raid Evacuation and Shelter Plan of the factory.

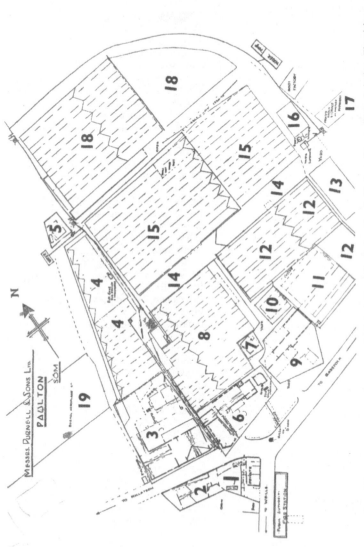

1. Mr. Purnell's house; offices; upper comp room. 2. Bristol Photo Engraving Co.; 3 Bindery, Case making, Jacketing, Electricians, Engineers. 4. New Stereo Plant; Sewing Room. 5. Fire Station 6. Stone Room, Reading Room, Keyboard Room. Mono Casters, Proof Room., Garage, Mono Mess Room. 7. Paint shop. 8. Packing Dept., Old Colour Room. 9. Farm House Offices, Garage. 10. Air Raid Shelter, (Nuts & Bolts). 11. Simmonds Aerocessories Ltd. (Nuts & Bolts). 12. Simmonds Aerocessories Ltd. (Nuts & Bolts). 13. Simmonds Aerocessories Ltd. (Canteen). 14. Passage (Temple Meads). 15. Machine Room; Colour Room, Folding Room, Stereo Room, Warehouse, Air Raid Shelter. 16. Boiler House. 17. Factory. 18. Offset Litho, Strong Room. 19. Bristol Aeroplane Co.

INDEX

A

Adnett David 227, 229,
Aga Khan 171,
Alderton Bert 175
Alfred Arnold Montague 183, 217,
Allied Type Founders (ATF) 135, 186
Almanac (Purnells) 24
Aly Khan 171
Andrews Chris 264,
Andy Pandy 126
Animal Cut-out Books 32
Archer Catherine 207,
Ariel Ltd. 215,
Army & Navy Stores 32
Articles of Association 38
Ascot Gold Cup 171,

B

Babcock Press 17,
Bailey David 174, 217,
Bamford J. 208,
Banfield Stella 50, 52,
Barnett Percy 46,
Barrow Paper Mills 117, 153, 209,
Barter Jean 121,
Bartlet Fred
Barton W. 215,
Bateson Ken 175,
Batt P 120,
Baylis Ebenezer 27,
Beacham Gert 121,
Beale George 105,
Beatrice Blocking Machine 28,
Beese Richard 267,
Bell George & Sons Ltd.
Bell Michael 215,
Bennet Bob 231,
Bennet Reg, 43,
Bentley H. G. 212,
Bently Arnold 212,
Berlin-Neuroder Kunstanstalten
Aktiengeselschaft 59,
Bird Bros. Ltd. 153,
Bird-in-Hand Tavern Pensford 7,
Birmingham Post & Mail 94,
Birn Bros. 58, 61,
Birn Monty 55,
Birn Morris 55,
Bisgrove Vic 44,
Bishop Victor 144, 166, 180,

Biss Richard 43,
Black A.C. 32,
Blake Ivy 52,
Blisset Roland 43,
Blitz 90,
Blomfield House 132,
Blyton Enid 104-109,
Board of Trade 63,
Boiler House,
Bond Nigel de M. OBE 89,
Book Centre 190-197,
Boon Eric 35,
Bourton Austin 29,
Box Joyce 52,
BPC Publishers 189,
BPCC 252,
Bradban Mr. 55, 74,
Braunmuller Rudolph 65,
Brehmer Sewing Machines 28, 117 (Folder),
123, 228,
Brice John 44,
Bridges Wally 43,
Briers Tom 46,
Bristol 18,
Bristol & North Somerset Railway 8, 9,
Bristol Aeroplane Company 75,
Bristol Photo Engraving 18, 58, 93,
British Board & Paper Mills 116,
British Greeting Cards 88, 215,
British Printing Company 264,
British Printing Corporation Ltd. 150-151,
Brooks Harold 44,
Brooks John Richard Uren 30. 43, 277,
Brooks William 45,
Brown K. R. 217, 226, 229, 264,
Bucksmere Ltd. 252, 254,
Budwig Dagobert 55, 59-60,
Budwig Stephan 56,59,
Bugden Eric 143, 174,
Bugle Press Ltd. 153,
Bull Netta 52,
Burge Albert 44,
Bush Harry 47,
Bushell Brian 228,
Butler's Boot Factory 21, 22, 29,

C

Cable Vision 248,
Camco folding machine 28,48,120,
Camelot Press 78,
Cameron Geoffrey 131,
Carey Alf 175,
Carpenter Charles 143,144, 174,

292

Fear Albert Edward 30, 92,
 Fear Reg 46,
Fear-Evans-Hill Mineral Railway 7,
Fell & Briant 146,
Ferbrache Mr. 6,
Filer Nora 52,
Film Review 66,
Finding Out Series 126,
Fire at Purnells 84,
Flexiback Machine (BMC) 124,
Flint David 43,
Flook 5, 22, 29,
Flook Joseph 4, 9,
Fooks Gwen 121,
Football Team 276,
Fowler H. 175,
Foyle Christina 72,
Foyle W & G Ltd. 86,
Freidheim Scoring machine 28,
Fricker George Herbert 30,
Furnival Press 27,
Futura Paperbacks 215

G

Gale & Polden Ltd. 146, 154,
Galleon Printers Ltd. 168,
Galliner Peter 199,
Geoghan (Pop) 119,
German Imports 62,
Gibbs John Clifford 25, 26, 27, 28, 31, 37, 38,
77, 78, 80, 101, 131, 150, 162, 186,
Gilchrist Bros. Ltd. 60,
Gillard Alfred 43,
Gillet Sir Harold 131,
Goddard Alfred 53,
Gollancz Victor 72, 74,
Goodman Terry 227, 229, 260, 264,
Grainger Alan 174, 231,
Grant A. C. 186,
Gravure Printing 73, 117,
Great Western Railways 6,
Green Harry (Publishers) Ltd. 88,
Greenhill David 71,
Gregory Wendy 168,
Greyfriars Ltd. 94,
Grigg William 39, 59,
Groves Len 43,

H

Hale Robert & Co. 41, 42,
Hallatrow 18,
Hancock Ken 43,

Hand Keith 231,
Hand V. 52,
Hardie Sir Charles 179-180, 206, 210, 217,
Harlequins Rugby Club 25,
Harley Mills 158,
Harrap & Co. Ltd. 32,
Harris Press Co. 32, 60, 103, 116, 120, 186,
Harris-Seybold-Potter Co. 34, 35,
Hart John 245, 248,
Hart L.A. 131,
Harvey A. J. (Bert) 40, 76,
Harvey Betty 81, 100,
Harvey Charles 109-110, 217,
Harvey Eric 81, 101, 102, 131, 144, 150, 162,
172, 174, 186, 210, 215,
Harvey Geoffrey 81, 149,
Harvey Judith 29,
Harvey Maurice 29, 175, 231,
Harvey W.J. (Bill) 145, 174, 175, 186, 187,
189, 210, 212,
Harvey Wilfred 5, 18, 19, 25, 27, 30, 31, 32,
33, 37, 84, 101, 131, 145, 150, 164, 165, 168,
211,
Harvey William Frederick (Fred) 29, 30, 75,
84, 101, 108, 116,
Hassell O.P. 217, 219, 224,
Hazell Sun Group 146-147,
Hazell Sun Ltd. 151,
Hazell Watson & Viney Ltd. 151, 213,
Hazells Offset Ltd. 151,
Heal Stanley 44,
Hewish Mick 175,
Hewitt Charles 1, 5, 38,
Hewitt Maria !,
Hewitt Sara 1,
High Life 210,
High Park Paulton 2,
Hildersley Henry Ltd. 101, 153,
Hill H. 16,
Hill John 6,
Hillman Queenie 274
History of the 20th. Century 211,
Hoare Julian 95,
Hodgson Roy 211, 226, 237,
Holloran John 235,
Holme Richard 184,196, 199,
Honeybun 125,
Hooke J.W. 226, 237,
Horne Captain Roderick 32, 33, 35, 36, 55,
Hounsell Eddie 211
Howard Frank 30,
Howe Bert 45,
Huber Press 20,
Hunt Stan 43,
Hunter Edward 70

I

IBM Computer 188,
Iliffe Edward Mauger 93, 94,
Iliffe William Coker 93,
Ink Factory (gravure) 177,
International Learning Systems Corporation 199- 07, 215,
Ireland Ernest 189,
Ivor Nicholson & Watson Ltd. 32,

J

Jackson John 224,
Jackson Stanley E. 39, 59,
James Bert 48,
Janes Publishing 218,
Jarvis Jack 170,
Jarvis Olive 52,
Jenkins Herbert Ltd. 32,
Jenkins Jessie 52,
Jephcott E.C. 95,
Job Losses 225,
Jones P. 30, 47,
Jones Tony 228,
Jones Tristan 144,
Juvenile Productions Ltd. 39, 88,

K

Kayebon Press Ltd. 168,
Kearton Lord 223,
Keliher Hudson & Kearns 152,
Kenny Terence 211,
Key & Whiting 11, 153,
Keys Bill 224,
Killen Maria 4,
Kingman P. 121,
Kings Norton Lord 185, 211,
Knowledge 134,
Koenig & Bauer 228,
Kolbus Binding Machines 228,
Krause Step & Repeat Machine 66,

L

Laidler Ron 228,
Langford 7,
Lanning Charlie 43,
Lavington P.A. (Hugh) 208, 217, 226, 239, 240, 244,

Lavington Peter 81, 100, 142, 162, 166, 170, 174, 186, 187, 210,
Le Bas Hedly 204,
Leroy 60,
Linotype Co.Ltd. 37, 143, 186,
Litho. Transparencies 66,
Lithoprinter 207,
Lockyear Fred 48,
Lunt Colin N. 231,

M

M.A.N. Sheetfed 5 col, 228,
M.A.N. Web Offset 207,
Mabbet & Edge 16,
Macdonald Publishing 103,
Macdonald T.T.& Co.Ltd. 88,
Macdonald Theodore 41,
Macmillan & Co.Ltd. 32, 74,
Magic Painting Books 56,
Mail Order Catalogues 127-128, 241, 244,
Maitland Adam 89,
Manor Farm Estate 9, 16, 20, 22, 31, 209,
Marshal Morgan & Scott 32, 73,
Marshall Howard 73,
Marshall Norman 199,
Marshall Peter 231,
Martini Perfect Binding 213,
Mason Don 211,
Masterman Richard 215,
Mathews Les 175,
Maxwell Communication Corporation (MCC) 252, 254-259,
Maxwell Ian 249,
Maxwell Robert 199, 217, 223, 224, 225, 226, 227, 232, 233, 236, 239, 246, 249, 253, 261,
May Lord 170,
Mayne Rev. C.C. 6, 12,
McBennet Michael 210, 217, 222, 226,
McDonald Film Laminator 103,
McIntosh Donald 175, 187, 189, 214, 217,227, 238,
Medlicott Sir Frank M.P. 66,
Meihle Presses 17, 27, 28, 69,
Melhuish Thomas 16,
Methuen & Co. Ltd. 32, 72,
Miall Dr. 29,
Mickey Mouse 33,
Midsomer Norton 2, 12, 13, 23,
Milk Marketing Board 213, 214,
Miller Mick 250,Maxwell Kevin 251,
Millward H 7,
Milverton Don 175, 196,
Minall Evelyn 52,

Q

Queenie (See Hillman)

R

S

T

GPO

PAPER NOVELTIES LI

DIRECTORS: W. GRIGG. S. E. JACKSON, E. J. UPPERTON

LUDGATE HOUSE

IS 35 ALLPURPOSE

ER PAULTON

Ariel Productions Ltd

DONALD MUNRO, M.A.LL

23-24 MAI

TELEPHONE: TEMPLE B

17/12/1991 5:08:33PM

HEAR THAT YOU

BIRTHDAY

S AND GOOD

THE MACDONALD

MACDON

RUNPRINT Ltd.

THE PACKAGING DIVISION OF THE PURNELL GROUP

Ltd.

ERS

KOMLOSY, MANAGING DIRECTOR
SECRETARY

on, E.8

tember, 1963

RUNPRINT LTD

THE PACKAGING DIVISION
OF THE PURNELL GROUP

PAULTON

NEAR

TELEPHO

PRINTERS : MANUFACTURERS OF WAXED PAPER : LAMINATED FOILS : CONVERTERS OF TRANS

Our Ref: MAG/SJH

LONDON OFFICE:
3. LUDGATE HILL · LONDON · E · C · 4
ELEPHONE: CITY 2665/6/7

WORKS:

PAULTON · NEAR BRISTOL

SOMERSET

TELEPHONE: MIDSOMER NORTON 3301/7

er 2nd 1956

"Convoy" Card
Game

TELEPHONE: MAYfair

PHILMAR

AMEX

Manufact